striped bass flies

# striped bass flies

## patterns of the pros

*Learn Where, When, and What to Use
to Catch the World's Most Popular
Saltwater Game Fish*

david klausmeyer

editor of *Fly Tyer* magazine

The Countryman Press

Woodstock, Vermont

ISBN 978-0-88150-731-7

Cover and interior photos by the author unless otherwise specified
Book design and composition by Carol J. Jessop, Black Trout Design

Published by The Countryman Press, P.O. Box 748, Woodstock, Vermont 05091

Distributed by W. W. Norton & Company, Inc., 500 Fifth Ave., New York, NY 10110

Printed in China

10 9 8 7 6 5 4 3 2 1

# contents

# introduction

"Let's talk about striped bass flies."

That's an interesting opening line for a book, isn't it? As you will see, however, it sets the perfect tone for this one. This isn't an ordinary book about flies. You know the kind I mean: pages of photos of flies with recipes, and perhaps a sentence or two describing how to use each pattern. I call those "fly encyclopedias," and they have their place. I just think a book about flies can be much more than that.

Over the years, I've written several books and hundreds of articles about fly tying and fishing. I'm also the editor of *Fly Tyer* magazine, and work with many of the best tiers in the world. All of these experiences have taught me that without including a healthy dose of fishing—when and where to use the flies, ideas about tackle selection, and any special fishing techniques—that a fly-tying book or article falls short of its ultimate goal, which is to help the reader catch fish.

Sure, this book contains about 90 terrific patterns designed to catch striped bass, but it also includes a wealth of information about where and when to fish on both the East and West Coasts. All of this information comes from interviews with thirteen of the best guides and fly designers in the business. These experts tell us how they tie flies, and how they catch the world's most popular saltwater fly-fishing game fish. Let me describe for you how this came about.

At the beginning of this project, I contacted a dozen or so guides who I knew had years of experience on the water and good reputations for being inventive fly tiers. These guides lived along the entire eastern Striped Bass Coast and California. I wanted to get as much geographic diversity as possible to better understand the full palette of opportunities to fish for stripers. I requested that they send samples of their flies, fill out a questionnaire describing the materials used to create their patterns, and include a few photos of themselves or clients that I could use for publication in this book. Most responded to my request, but if a guide did not reply, I contacted another from his general area to take his place. In the end, I had a list of thirteen fly-fishing and tying experts who I knew would have a lot to say about fly tying and fishing for striped bass.

The next step was to conduct taped interviews with the guides. We talked about the prevalent forms of bait in their areas, the length of their fishing seasons, tackle recommendations, and other important pieces of information that would help a visiting angler catch striped bass and occasionally other species of game fish. At some point during our conversations, I would ask, "let's talk about your flies." This is when the guides shared their theories of fly design and construction, and gave specific details on how to fish with their patterns.

The chapters are arranged to follow the natural progression of the fishing season along what I call the eastern Striped Bass Coast. We begin our journey on North Carolina's Outer Banks with Capt. Brian Horsley. We then move north to Chesapeake Bay and meet Capt. Chris Newsome. Two terrific guides—Captains Gene Quigley and Joe Mustari—share their professional insights to fishing the New Jersey shore. Capt. Joe Blados represents New York, and tells us the history of his famous topwater pattern, the Crease Fly. Capt. Jim Ellis, a descendant of a passenger on the *Mayflower,* puts the real meaning in the term "home waters" when he discusses fishing for striped bass around Cape Cod. Capt. Lynne Heyer shares her extensive knowledge of fishing the flats and harbors of Nantucket Island. We get the skinny on fishing Rhode Island from my good friend Capt. Ray Stachelek. We then end our journey up the Striped Bass Coast in Maine, with Captains Eric Wallace and Doug Jowett.

Next, we'll hop over to California and meet Capt. Dan Blanton. Dan fishes the San Francisco Bay area, and proves that there are good opportunities to fish for striped bass on both coasts. A slightly different version of this interview appeared in *Fly Tyer* magazine, but the version in this book contains a different set of flies as well as some great photos of a couple of monster bass.

When I started this project, I planned to include only guides. I wanted to get the perspective of the folks who stake their livelihoods on the flies they tie and recommend to their clients. Along the way, however, I discovered two tiers who I thought would make fine additions to this book. The first is Joe O'Clair, who runs a company on Cape Cod called Flycatcher Saltwater Flies. Joe started his business several years ago, and has created a number of very interesting patterns. In addition to talking about fly design and fishing, we also discussed what it takes to start a small fly tying business.

And finally, you'll meet New York's David Nelson. David ties Flat-wing patterns that take much of their inspiration from classic Spey River Atlantic salmon flies. Yes, you read that correctly: It's sort of the Spey River meets Joppa Flats. His patterns are amazing to behold, and they will get you excited about tying and experimenting at the vise. And, in a sport populated with old farts—like me— David Nelson brings an exciting, youthful perspective to fly-fishing.

This is obviously only a very short list of the people who are creating superb flies for catching striped bass. Your favorite guide or fly designer might not be on the list. I know this will disturb— perhaps even anger—some critics. Well, I had two choices. In the first, I could compile yet another encyclopedia of fly patterns, and include only the best-known fly tiers. Or second, I could devote more space to talking with the tiers about fly design and fishing, and introduce you to some new people who deserve recognition for their excellent work. I chose the latter, and believe that this book features a lot of excellent flies *and* contains a wealth of information that you can use to catch striped bass. And along the way, you'll meet a couple of folks who are making exciting contributions to fly tying and fishing.

See you on the water!
—*David Klausmeyer*
The coast of Maine
May 2007

# The OBX
## with Capt. Brian Horsley

1

A lot of anglers think that the Northeast is home to the best fly-fishing for striped bass on the East Coast. But there's more to striper fishing than just Long Island and Cape Cod. There are excellent opportunities all along the eastern seaboard.

The coast of North Carolina is a hot spot for salt-water fly-fishing. Anglers in this area also enjoy a very long season; Captains Brian Horsley and Sara Gardner are swinging into action when Northeast fishermen are stoking logs on the fire, tying flies, and dreaming about spring.

Captains Brian Horsley and Sara Gardner are a rare husband-and-wife guide team. I've heard of such partnerships guiding in freshwater destinations, but never on the salt. They are experts at the sport, and also very accomplished tiers. And, to succeed in the unique nature of the striper fishery along the Outer Banks, commonly known as the OBX, they have developed a series of patterns and fishing techniques to reach the largest bass hanging in some very deep water.

Are you a really serious Northeast striped bass aficionado? Then spend your regular season—spring through autumn—whacking at the stripers in your home water. Then, when winter comes, travel south to the Outer Banks. It's a great way to beat the winter doldrums and enjoy some really fine fishing.

I enjoyed a wide-ranging conversation with Capt. Horsley. He started by filling me in about where he fishes.

"We fish the northern Outer Banks of North Carolina out of the Oregon Inlet, which takes in Nags Head, Kitty Hawk, and that general area. We can cover a lot of territory to find fish."

How long have you guys been guiding?

"I've been guiding for sixteen years, and she's been guiding for ten or eleven. There might be some other husband-and-wife guide teams, but I've never heard of one, at least not saltwater guides."

Yes, there are very few husband-and-wife guide teams. So how does it work? Are you on the same boat, or different boats?

"Yeah, we're pretty unique that way. We both have twenty-three-foot Jones Brothers. We often guide on the same days, which is helpful because we stay in contact by radio and let each other know where we're finding fish. Most guides play it pretty close to the vest, but we can keep each other informed, which is also a benefit to the client."

What's the season for striped bass in the Outer Banks?

"Our fly-fishing season for striped bass starts in mid-December—depending on how cold it gets—and runs until the first of March. The fish are coming down the coast. About eighty percent of the migrating stripers winter off the coast of North Carolina. They arrive in waves from mid-December through January. January is the peak month."

So, if a guy is really into catching striped bass, he can fish in the Northeast until about mid-November, and then follow the bass down to you.

"That's right. We keep very busy starting in December, but weather is definitely a factor. It's all ocean fishing, and the Oregon Inlet is one of the three worse inlets for rough seas on the East Coast."

So, you're fishing on the outside of the banks?

"Yes, it's all in the ocean. We fish right along the beach. You can't go out more than three miles, anyway, because of the Magnuson-Stevens Act. The federal waters are closed to striper fishing. We're fishing from right along the beach to water that is about sixty feet deep."

You're obviously fishing a variety of conditions. What sort of tackle do you use?

"It's primarily a sinking-line fishery. You can catch them rolling on top, but you'll always find the bigger

*Half & Half Super-Size*

bass in deeper water. If I'm freezing my butt off in the winter, I want the biggest bass I can catch. We prefer a 450-grain sinking head. I especially like that Rio T-14 head. It's perfect. I use a five- to six-foot-long leader of straight twenty-pound-test monofilament. It's not about making lots of casts, the technique is to make a cast and then count until the fly reaches the proper depth where you're catching the bigger fish."

What type of fish show up first: schoolies or big bass?

"The first bass are always really big fish. They're hard to find—there aren't as many of them—but by the first to the middle of December, we get some really nice fish. One day Sara caught seven bass on flies that each weighed more than thirty-two pounds. The biggest one was right at forty pounds. She called me, and I got there just as the bite was ending, but the guys in my boat caught three bass that each weighed in the mid-thirties. That's not a bad day of fishing!"

What size rod do you normally recommend?

"A ten weight. That will work just fine."

Capt. Horsley emphasized the differences between fishing the Outer Banks and the popular Northeast striped bass fisheries.

"It's a really world-class fishery, but the Outer Banks is different from what you'll see up north. It's a little deeper water, and you're fishing to bait with only a few rolling fish. Mainly you're fishing to the bait."

What are the most common species of bait?

"Primarily bunker, but last year we had tons of round herring. When the water gets a little warmer we get round herring. We also get a shot of blueback herring, but they're in terrible trouble so you don't see that many. And we get bay anchovies in the later part of the season; when the Bonaparte gulls show up, you know they're on the anchovies."

You sent some great flies. They're really well tied. But man, a couple of them are pretty large. You like big flies, don't you?

"Well, our bait is big. The bunker can be up to twelve and fourteen inches long. But when the bait is running smaller, you can use a small Half & Half, like the fly I call Sara's Half & Half. That pattern does a good job of matching a four- or five-inch-long bunker."

What do you think is the most important aspect of creating a good striped bass fly?

"I find that the profile of the fly doesn't make that much difference. I think the length of the fly is the most important consideration. And what we do is

*Deceiver*

*Half & Half*

imitate a jig. We learned that from the heathen; the best old-time striper bait around here is a three-ounce jig with a six-inch Twister tail. So hell, why not design a fly that looks and acts like that. When the bunker get bigger, we use longer flies. And if you use a fly that can get down fifty feet, you're going to find a really big bass. You'll see them on the depth finder down to seventy feet deep, but they're also up as high as twenty-five feet. It's pretty easy to get to that depth. Other times, when they're close to the beach, they'll be in water that is fifteen feet of water."

Do you ever fish from the beach?

"When the beach fishing is good and I'm not guiding, sure, we'll fish from the beach. On Christmas day last year, Sara and I did real well from the beach using flies. They were ten- to twenty-five-pound fish. And they were thick. But when guiding, we fish from boats so we can move to find fish."

What other species do you fish for?

"We guide for stripers from December until the first of March, but we fish three hundred days a year. At the end of April, we go for big bluefish and speckled trout, but there are also some schoolie bass. I use Hi-Tie Clousers for bluefish and bass in the spring. In the summer, we have speckled trout and catch a lot of black-tipped sharks on flies. We also have cobia, and on some years we have really good redfish action."

Your striped bass fishing sounds quite different from what the guys are doing in the Northeast. Up the coast, it's more common to fish from beaches. Overall, it sounds like you fish slightly offshore in deeper water.

"Yes, people get baffled when they come down here because it's not like what they find in New England in the summer. They ask, 'where are the stripers in the surf?' I tell them that if that's what they're looking for then they should go up north. But then they start catching our big fish, and they're happy."

### Kreh/Clouser Half & Half

**Hook:** Regular stainless-steel hook such as the Mustad 34007, size 4/0.

**Thread:** Danville's Flat Waxed Nylon, white.

**Tail:** Two to three pairs of 5- to 6-inch-long white saddle hackles and strands of pearl Flashabou.

**Belly:** Red bucktail.

**Back:** Gray bucktail with strands of pearl Krystal Flash.

**Eyes:** Large aluminum dumbbell eyes with dome eye inserts. These eyes add only a modest amount of weight so you can still cast the fly, and they are good imitations of large bunker eyes.

**Note:** This is Sara's "go-to" striper fly; her clients have taken many fish weighing more than 30 pounds using this fly. Blane Choclate, a friend and talented tier, showed her this fly. You may tie this general pattern in your choice of colors to match your local fishing conditions.

### Kreh/Clouser Half & Half Super-Size

**Hook:** Gamakatsu SL 12, size 4/0.

**Thread:** Danville's Flat Waxed Nylon, olive or chartreuse.

**Tail:** Five to six pairs of 7- to 10-inch-long saddle hackles. For fishing clear water, use a fly tied with chartreuse and white feathers; gray, mauve and orange work best for dirty water.

**Belly:** Bucktail, color to complement the tail.

**Back:** Bucktail and strands of Flashabou or Krystal Flash, colors to complement the tail.

**Eyes:** Heavy lead eyes.

**Note:** These flies are tied full and fished when the bass are feeding on big bunker. The heavy eyes make them a favorite for fishing deep, especially when the fish are holding along the beach.

### Lefty's Deceiver Super Sized #1

**Hook:** Gamakatsu SL 12, size 4/0.

**Thread:** Danville's Flat Waxed Nylon, olive.

**Tail:** Two pairs of mauve, gray saddles, and white saddle hackles. These feathers can be up to 8 inches long. Add a few strands of pearl Flashabou.

**Belly:** Red bucktail.

**Back:** Red, white, olive, and brown bucktail.

**Eyes:** Large pearl dome eyes glued to the sides of the head.

**Note:** Be sure to tie a bunch of bucktail on each side of the fly to keep the long hackles from fouling around the hook.

## TIER'S TUTORIAL: *Tying the Half & Half*

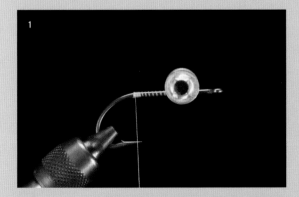

Start the thread on the hook. Tie on the dumbbell eyes.

Tie on six saddle hackles in your choice of colors. Place three feathers on each side of the tail; the two halves of the tail should curve together.

(tying steps continue on the next page)

You may wish to tie on a few pieces of flash material.

Tie on bunches of bucktail at the base of the tail.

Tie on a bunch of red bucktail to form the belly of the fly. This is another area where you can experiment and substitute with other colors of bucktail.

Tie on a bunch of bucktail to form the back of the fly.

Tie a few strands of flash material to the top of the fly. Wrap the thread behind the base of the eyes to compress the bucktail and form a stream-lined silhouette. Wrap the thread in front of the eyes to form a neat head, tie off and clip the thread, and coat the thread wraps with cement.

# Capt. Chris Newsome
# Fishes Chesapeake Bay

2

*I*'ll never forget the first time I fished Chesapeake Bay; it was a truly memorable experience. To be more specific, I fished the Potomac River, which is a tributary to the Chesapeake. I was attending a fly-fishing show in the Washington D.C. area, and a friend named Rick, who was a part-time guide at the time, asked if I would like to go fishing that evening. I had spent the entire day tying flies and entertaining a large crowd, and could use a few hours on the water to unwind.

Rick and I drove to the end of National Airport where there was a nice parking lot and boat ramp at the end of one of the runways. The commercial jets were flying so low that we could actually feel the wind as they passed overhead. (In this post-9/11 world, I would be surprised to learn that that boat ramp and parking lot still exist.) My friend quickly launched his boat, and we were soon flying upriver.

It was a magnificent trip. Along the way, we passed the Washington and Jefferson Memorials, and many other important landmarks; it was a unique way to get a tour of our nation's capital. We continued up the Potomac, passing the clubhouses of several crew teams. Eventually, the banks along the river became very steep and heavily wooded. Rick cut the motor and said "Let's fish."

In addition to large numbers of schoolie-size bass, the river was full of hickory and American shad. We spent a pleasant couple of hours catching stripers, all weighing three to five pounds apiece. After a while, Rick pulled out a fly rod with a full-sinking line and offered me shad flies. "Try this," he said. Even the shad were in a taking mood, and I quickly caught three or four.

"Want to catch a really big striper?" Rick asked.
"Sure."
"Then catch another shad."

After a few minutes, I had a two-pound hickory shad on the line.

"Give him here," he said.

I handed the fish to Rick. He then pulled a small spinning rod out of the hold in the hull of the boat. He tied about a size 4/0 bait hook to the end of the line, impaled the hook into the lip of the shad, and tossed the fish overboard. Rick then sat on the edge of the boat, his feet dangling in the water.

Every so often, I could see the tip of the rod bob

up and down from the pressure of the excited shad below. After about five minutes, the entire rod rocketed toward the water like a divining rod.

"I've got a big one!"

Sure enough, Rick was in a tug of war with a very large striped bass. His small rod really wasn't designed for this heavy task, but Rick put up a very good fight. After about 10 minutes, he hauled a fat, 20-pound striper into the boat.

"I wonder what happened to the shad," I mused.

We peered into the gullet of the fish, but found nothing. We glanced overboard, and then looked at the belly of the big striper.

"I can only wonder," Rick said.

Yes, the entire Chesapeake Bay and its tributaries is one of the finest fly-fishing destinations on the Atlantic seaboard. Unfortunately, work has taken my friend to another part of the country. But don't worry: There are other expert guides who are eager to show you the rhythms of this magnificent fishery. Capt. Chris Newsome is one of those guides. He is a full-time guide specializing in saltwater fly-fishing. Capt. Newsome has spent his entire life learning the Chesapeake and its fish. During our interview, I learned that my unique experience with the shad and that big striper was just a sampling of the amazing fishing we can enjoy on the Chesapeake.

"I've been fishing all of my life. I grew up on the Chesapeake Bay. My father and I spent a lot of time on the water, doing a lot of light tackle stuff. Fly-fishing is definitely getting a lot bigger around here. When I was young, however, very few people fly-fished. It's really catching on."

Where exactly do you live and fish?

"I live in Gloucester County. That's north of the Norfolk/Virginia Beach area. I fish in two different areas and fisheries. I fish in what we call the Middle Peninsula area. That's more protected water, and a little shallower. It's about three to five feet of water. We catch a variety of fish in the shallows: striped bass, speckled trout, and puppy drum, which are redfish."

I didn't know there were redfish in your area.

"We're kind of at the northern edge of their range; it depends upon water temperature and probably some other factors. The numbers of redfish and the quality of the fishing can be cyclical, but it gives

us some nice variety. Last week, actually, we went down to the Virginia Beach area; there's a little population that holds in there all winter long. The water was about fifty degrees, and we were catching redfish."

What's the season for fishing for striped bass in the Chesapeake Bay?

"Depending upon the weather, it may never end. In the peninsula area, that area we're talking about right now, we are fishing eel grass flats, oyster bars, creek mouths, rock piles, and other structure like that. That's all shallow-water fishing. But typically, that fishing runs from May until mid-November. The fish will then move out of the shallow water and begin schooling up in the main waters of the bay."

Your area is especially known for having big striped bass. When do they show up?

"Yes, we also get the big migratory fish. Those start showing up sometime Thanksgiving. They'll be here through around the first of April. But that's open-water fishing. This past year, we had a great December and January for the big trophy bass. And we have lots of fish. February, however, can be kind of tough depending upon the weather. March can also be kind of if tough to fish. But then the fishing picks up again in April. It all depends upon the weather, and some seasons we can fish all year long."

I once attended the Old Dominion Fly Fishing Show. I don't think that show exists anymore, which is too bad because it was very good. Anyway, a local guide asked if I wanted to go fishing that night. We started about midnight and fished until four in the morning. All I really remember is that the guide shoved us off from the boat launch, we floated under a big bridge, and spent the night catching fish. I mean, we caught a striper on almost every cast. It was one of those silly times when you start trying every fly in your box just to see if you could find something that *wouldn't* work. I mean, *everything* caught fish, and the water boiled with stripers. Do you do much night fishing, and do you ever encounter those sorts of conditions?

"March can be kind of tough, like I said, so sometimes we'll do some night fishing under the tunnel bridges. Yeah, we'll do it right under the bridge. You can see the fish swimming around. We'll look for what we call the light line; that's the shadow line

*Breathing Baitfish*

*Bay Juvie*

formed by the lights from the bridge. The fish lay right on that shadow line, in the transition from light to dark. You can see the fish swimming in the line; they lay on the dark side and wait for bait to come into the light. We come up behind the fish and sight cast to them. This is the only sort of real sight fishing that we have around here, but it's a lot of fun. It's at night, and it's really unique. It's also a great way to catch a lot of fish."

But what about when you're fishing in the shallow water? Are you sight fishing in the shallows?

"No, our water clarity is usually pretty poor. We don't get the water clarity we would need for any sort of consistent sight fishing. We get good conditions for sight fishing a few times in the year: the right wind, clear water—things like that. For the most part, we're blind fishing to structure and areas where we know the fish will be holding."

*Rock Candy Crab*

You sent a fly called the Rock Candy Crab. I thought this was a fly for sight fishing. I'm wrong about that?

"I use even that for fishing blind. In late October through November, we'll fish back in the marsh drain areas. The fish will stack up at the mouths of these drains and feed on the small blue crabs. They'll also feed on a variety of other crabs. Their bellies will be rock hard, full of crabs. I fish that fly with a dead drift, letting it swing slowly through the current coming out of the drain. You can also catch the fish

using Clouser Minnows and patterns like that; the fish aren't too particular. But, that little crab is sort of a fun fly. It's just something different to try."

*Spartina Grass Shrimp*

I'm also looking at your Spartina Grass Shrimp. That must be another shallow water or flats fly, right?

"Yes, that's another one we'll fish back in those marshy areas. The fish will be feeding on shrimp over the eel-grass flats and back in the marshes. But I also fish that fly blind."

What is the predominant bait in your area?

"In our area, the majority of our bass feed on baitfish such as menhaden and silversides, but a small part of their diet is made up of shrimp and especially crabs."

When do you switch over to fishing the more open water?

"We'll start seeing the smaller fish schooling up in the open water some time in October. You'll see breaking fish and a lot of bird action; the birds are the tip off. The fish will be in the open water all winter. But the big bass will start showing up some time around Thanksgiving. Generally, the better open-water fishing is down around the mouth of the bay. In the past, the big fish would come up into the bay, but lately we've been having a problem with the menhaden. You've probably heard about the harvesting of the menhaden. The menhaden are being over-harvested, and there's not enough bait to draw the big fish up into the bay; there's no reason for them to come up into the bay to feed."

Capt.Chris Newsome Fishes Chesapeake Bay   13

*Woolly Bully*

Do you use different types of tackle for fishing the shallow water versus fishing the open water?

"For the most part, when we're fishing the shallow water, we're targeting the schoolie striped bass and red-fish. Those bass can be twenty-eight to thirty inches long. I like to use a six-, seven- or eight-weight rod. We'll be fishing with intermediate-sinking lines. And we'll be using smaller flies—size 1 and 1/0 Clousers and flies like that. Nothing bigger than a size 2/0 fly. Once we get the bigger fish, we'll up the size of our tackle to an eight-, nine-, or ten-weight. For a lot of our open-water fishing, we'll use fast-sinking lines to get down quickly. The fish might be close to the surface, but then they'll drop down to water that is thirty feet deep.

"It's tough to target them that deep. Ideally, we hope that the fish will be up higher. But, there are times when we easily get them twenty feet down. When they're that deep, we use Rio T-14 shooting heads and heavily weighted Clousers and other patterns with a lot of weight."

*Tie 'Um High Bunker*

The Tie 'Um High Bunker is a beautiful pattern. Tell me about that fly.

"That's a great pattern for catching the bigger bass. It casts pretty easily, and it's a good match for the menhaden. I catch the majority of my big fish on that fly."

When you say big fish, how big are you talking about?

"Oh, this past year we had fish as large as forty-three inches. We had quite a few in the forty-inch range. But sometimes you can catch an eighteen-inch fish, and then turn right around and catch a forty-inch bass. It's a mix because we have the resident schoolie fish, but then we also get the big migratory fish. The big fish will over-winter and fatten up—they'll put on a lot of weight—and then spawn. The winter fish we get are real fat; sometimes it looks like they're going to explode. Some of them almost look like barrels. Sometimes they're feeding on really huge bait, but other times they are feeding on really small, one-inch-long silversides. We were out there one day at the end of January, and there were clouds of these little bay anchovies. There were so many they were turning the water black. You could see the big fish swimming through the bait with their mouths open. They were just scooping them up. That was a really neat day. In addition to all the bait and bass, the humpback whales were close to the boat. The whales come close to the mouth of the bay during the winter. That's pretty neat."

You sent only subsurface patterns. Do you ever fish topwater?

"Sometimes you can get them on poppers when they're really busting on top. But usually, ninety percent of the time, I fish with a fast-sinking line or shooting head. Even if the fish are close to the top, I'll still use a sinking line. I start stripping the fly as soon as it hits the water. The better fish generally don't take flies on top, but they will take a fly that's sinking. The smaller fish will work on top, and the bigger fish will be down below."

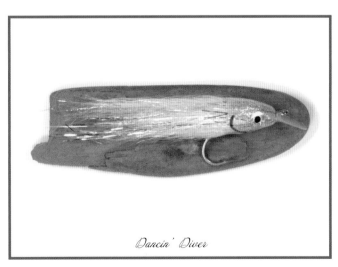

*Dancin' Diver*

The Dancin' Diver is a very cool fly. The lip must give it a lot of action.

"That's just something I've been playing around with. The lip makes it dive and gives it a lot of action, but the head is made of foam. What happens is, when you stop stripping the fly, it just sort of hangs in the water. Oftentimes the fish will hit it between strips. But the lip gives it a real erratic motion. It's something different for your fly box. I like it on days when it's real slow and I'm not catching fish."

What do you look for in a fly?

"There several things I look at. I think matching the size of the bait is the most important thing. The action of the fly is also very important. The Dancin' Diver, for instance, has an action that is totally different from any other fly out there. The exact color of the fly is probably the least important factor."

*Noisy Clouser*

The Noisy Clouser is a great fly. I'm going to tie this one in the book.

"You can add a rattle to a lot of flies. There are a lot of ways to do it. What's different about this pattern is that the rattle is well protected. One of the problems with tying the rattle on the belly of the fly is that when casting, you might smack the fly on the side of the boat and break the rattle. On the Noisy Clouser, the rattle is protected inside the Mylar tubing and is far less likely to get broken. You can use this method to add a rattle to almost any fly."

With the rattle, it must be an excellent night-time fly.

"Yes it is. I also use the Noisy Clouser in cloudy water. The visibility of the water in the bay is pretty low, and the rattle helps the fish find the fly. I tie that fly in a lot of colors: chartreuse, fire orange, and gold."

You say you can fish year around, but do you guide all year?

"Ideally, for fishing the shallow water in the more protected areas, October and November is a lot of fun. We have a lot of fish in the shallows, but there is also a lot of variety such as speckled trout and redfish. You can actually make three casts and catch three different species of fish: a striper, a trout, and a redfish. It's kind of a neat thing to do. There aren't a lot of areas where you have this sort of mixture of fish. It's a mixing ground between North and South."

What about fishing the open water and targeting the big fish? What's the best time for doing that?

"December or January are best. Again, however, it's dependent upon the weather and water temperature. This year, it was best in January; other years, it's best in December. It varies. Sometimes, if we get some warm days, we have great fishing in February. This year, because of the weather, I didn't guide at all in February; I started guiding again the middle of March."

It's early April now and you're already guiding.

"Oh yeah, we're catching plenty of fish. This time

of the year we do a lot of night fishing under the lights."

Do you get a lot of clients who want to go out at night?

"This time of year, it's the best way to consistently catch fish, so I try to push people to do that. We'll usually go out for four hours or so—time it with the tide and current. You want strong, moving water. You're almost guaranteed to catch fish. We then head back in after about four hours. It's a nice trip."

Near the end of our interview, I asked Chris how he got into guiding, and what he did in his off hours. Even when he's not fishing, he's thinking and even writing about fishing.

"I was managing a tackle shop and guiding part time. Between the two, it was running me ragged. I made a decision that I wanted to pursue guiding more, and I didn't know anyone in this area who was strictly a fly-fishing guide. I thought I'd give it a try as a full-time fly-fishing guide. It's also given me more time to work on my Web site and write a few articles for some magazines."

### Tie 'Um High Bunker

**Hook:** Tiemco TMC600SP or Mustad C68SSS, sizes 2 to 6/0.
**Thread:** Clear monofilament.
**Body:** Blended Silky Fiber and Angel Hair in pearl, pink, and olive. You may substitute with Mirror Image, Fuzzy Fiber, or yak hair. Use a black permanent marker to make the spot on the side of the body.
**Eyes:** Large white dome eyes.

### Noisy Clouser

**Hook:** Gamakatsu SC15, sizes 2 to 1/0.
**Thread:** Danville's Flat Waxed Nylon, chartreuse.
**Tail:** Chartreuse Krystal Flash.
**Body:** Bucktail and grizzly saddle hackle.
**Eyes:** Large chrome dumbbell with chartreuse dome eyes.
**Rattle:** Large rattle inside a piece of medium Mylar tubing.

### Woolly Bully Minnow

**Hook:** Gamakatsu SC15, sizes 2 to 1/0.

**Thread:** UTC gel-spun 100.
**Tail:** Green and white Polar Fiber, and silver Polar Flash.
**Body:** Olive and white wool. You may add stripes using a green permanent marker.
**Eyes:** Medium silver dome eyes.

### Bay Juvie

**Hook:** Gamakatsu SC15, sizes 1 to 2/0.
**Thread:** UTC gel-spun.
**Tail:** Grizzly over white hackles, and strands of pearl Krystal Flash.
**Body and head:** White marabou and white EP Fibers.
**Eyes:** Medium pearl dome eyes.

### Spartina Grass Shrimp

**Hook:** Mustad S71SSS, sizes 4 to 1.
**Thread:** Olive Danville's Flat Waxed Nylon.
**Antennae:** Pearl and black Krystal Flash.
**Head, tail and tail:** Slinky Fiber.
**Eyes:** Melted monofilament.
**Body:** Olive Estaz.

### Rock Candy Crab

**Hook:** Mustad S71SSS, sizes 4 to 1/0.
**Thread:** Olive Danville's Flat Waxed Nylon.
**Body:** Deer hair.
**Weight:** Soft lead, yellow acrylic paint, and epoxy.
**Eyes:** Melted monofilament.
**Claws:** Grizzly hackle clipped and dipped in Softex.
**Legs:** Grizzly Silli Legs.

### Dancin Diver

**Hook:** Mustad S71SSS, size 1/0.
**Thread:** Clear monofilament.
**Head:** A popper body placed on the hook shank with the pointed end facing forward. After tying the fly, coat the head with epoxy, Softex, or a similar material.
**Body:** Polar Flash or a similar material in your choice of colors.
**Eyes:** Medium adhesive eyes.
**Gills:** Red permanent marker.
**Lip:** Fly Lipp.

**Note:** To learn more about or to purchase Fly
Lipps, go to www.flylipps.com.

**Breathing Baitfish**
**Hook:** Mustad 79666S, size 1/0.
**Thread:** Red 3/0 (210 or 280 denier).
**Eyes:** Large dumbbell.
**Tail:** Splayed grizzly hackle and Polar Flash.
**Body:** White and chartreuse arctic fox.
**Gills:** Red arctic fox.

TIER'S TUTORIAL: *Tying the Noisy Clouser*

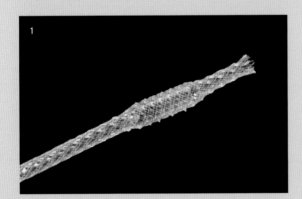

Insert a large rattle into a piece of EZ Body tubing.

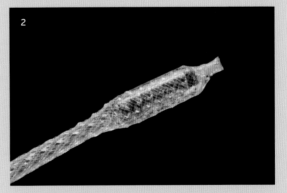

Tie off and clip the end of the tubing. Coat the
rattle and tubing with epoxy or cement.

(tying steps continue on the next page)

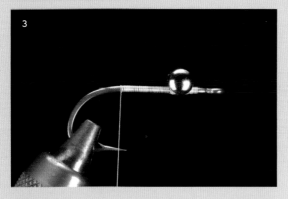

Start the thread on the hook. Tie on the dumbbell.

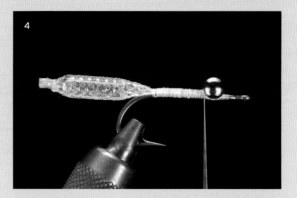

Tie the tubing to the top of the hook shank; the rattle should hang beyond the end of the hook.

Tie your choice of bucktail on top of the hook. Use enough bucktail to shroud the rattle.

I like to wrap tinsel or some sort of braided material up the hook shank to form the body of the fly.

Tie on your favorite colors of bucktail to form the back of the fly. Tie on your favorite colors and brand of flash material. Tie off and clip the thread. Coat the thread wraps with cement.

# The Jersey Shore
## with Capt. Gene Quigley

3

ew Jersey is synony-
mous with good fishing
for striped bass. There are
hundreds of miles of beach to
prowl, and countless inlets, bays and backwaters. And,
as we will learn, New Jersey enjoys a very long
fishing season. I think it's fair to say that if you are serious about traveling the Striper Coast, visiting New
Jersey must be near the top of your list.

One of the biggest problems I had in writing this
book was selecting one or two guides to represent
New Jersey; there are literally dozens of superb
guides and fly tiers fishing those waters. It's impos-
sible to include them all, so if your favorite guide is
not included, he's in very good company. Let me as-
sure you that there was no intent to slight anyone.

First, we will visit with Capt. Gene Quigley. He's
a pro at fishing central New Jersey, but he is a very
mobile guide and will move his base of operation
from central to northern New Jersey as the fish move
up the coast. Capt. Quigley is also a very good fly tier
who sticks to the tried and true patterns.

"I grew up on the Jersey shore" Capt. Quigley said
at the beginning of our interview. "Our house was
right on the ocean. When I was a kid, I fished and
crabbed and surfed and sailed. I've been fly-fishing for
about twenty-five years, and guiding for fifteen.

"I guide in Central New Jersey from the southern
end of Raritan Bay, along the outer beaches, down to
Barnegat Bay. I also do a lot of guiding in the spring
within the interior of Barnegat Bay."

When do you fish inside Barnegat Bay?

"We usually start around the beginning of April,
and continue working the backwaters until the end
of May to the first of June. Then we gear our efforts
toward the outer beaches as the bass move out of the
backwaters and run north."

What's drawing them inside the bay?

"It's all about bait and water temperature. A lot of
times there is a variety of bait spawning at the same
time. The four main baits are grass shrimp, spearing,
herring, and adult bunker. It's all there at the same time.

"The small bass start showing up around mid-
March, and really start pouring in around mid-April. As
soon as the herring start moving to the inside to spawn
in the streams and rivers, the big fish will also come in."

*Shrimp*

Since you're fishing in the backwater, do you do
any sight fishing?

"We have some sight fishing, but we're really
fishing the transitions from the shallow to the deeper
water. We look for currents and drop-offs. A lot of
times, the way our backwaters are set up, the bait is
getting swept off the flats into the deeper holes and
drop-offs. I'm looking for transitions from two to four
feet dropping off to as deep as eighteen to twenty
feet. Depending upon the moon, we can have a six-
to eight-foot tide swing, but that's to the extreme;
we're usually looking at a three- to four-foot tide.

"Barnegat Bay is a big system. The backwater is
seventy-five-square miles, and it all gets pushed in
through a half-mile-wide inlet. We get a tremendous
tide flow pushing on the east side of the bay, and the
fluctuation isn't as great as we work toward the west
side of the bay."

What kind of lines do you use to fish the backwater?

"We use all three—a floating, an intermediate,
and a sinking line, depending upon the situation.
When we do fish the flats, we generally don't sight
fish. Our conditions don't allow for a lot of sight
fishing. First, most of it has a muddy, dark colored
bottom. The flats that contain sand are eelgrass flats.
On a really calm day we will see tailing striped bass."

Are you fishing subsurface or with surface flies?

"We do a lot of teasing with topwater poppers.
Sometimes we fish with a big Bob's Banger, but other
times I'll cast a large hookless popping plug with a
light spinning rod. If you cast a big chugger, you'll
raise some very nice fish, especially bigger bass. I'll
chug that thing as we're drifting across the mud or

*Baby Angel*

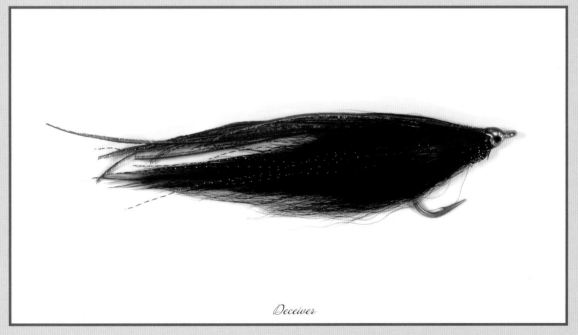

*Deceiver*

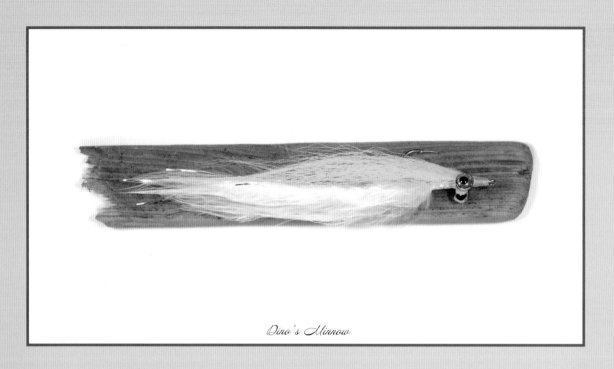

*Dino's Minnow*

*Half & Half*

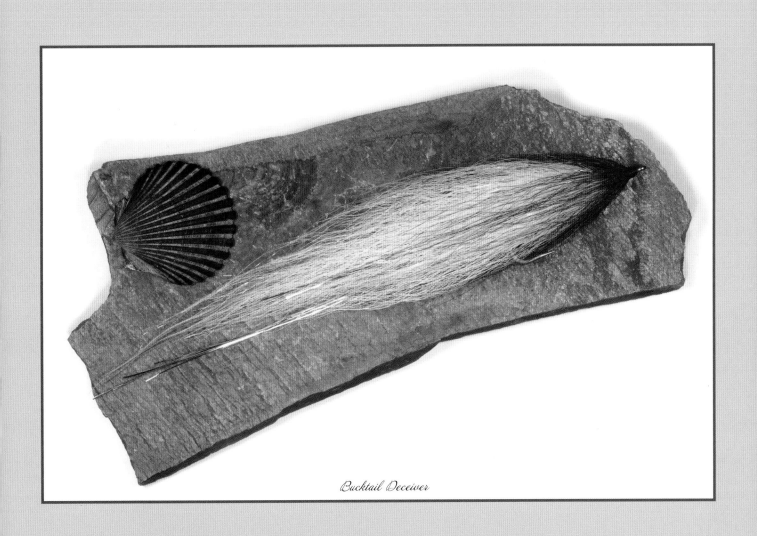

*Bucktail Deceiver*

*Bob's Banger*

eelgrass, and you'll see swirling fish behind it. I'll get the fish up, and then pull in the plug and let the client cast right in with a Banger. I can usually get the fish pretty close to the boat and within casting range."

Do you ever find that a loud popper spooks the fish, especially when they're in the shallows?

"There are times when we'll drift over an area, and I'll see the fish tailing and know there's a school of bass around. Now I probably won't use that big chugger in fear of spooking those fish. I'll just let the client cast into the direction of the drift and the tailing fish."

What kind of flies do you use early in the season?

"We use a lot of Surf Candies early in the year, particularly when there are a lot of spearing in the water. We'll have years in the back of Barnegat—and

*Surf Candy*

also in Raritan Bay—when there are a lot of spearing. The spearing spawn in March and April. We get a lot of big spearing early in the spring, and as the spring progresses we go right down to very, very small spearing about the size of a dime or quarter. Those small spearing will grow and mature throughout the year. The smallest Surf Candy I'll use is maybe an inch and a half to two inches long."

What is the most important type of bait in your area?

"Spearing and bunker stay with us all year long. Those are the two critical main baits that we have throughout the season. Now, with respect to bunker, it depends upon the time of year whether we have the really big bunker or the little peanut bunker. And again, the time of year determines if we have six- to eight-inch spearing or the one- to two-inch spearing. With both the spearing and bunker, we get the bigger bait early in the season."

When do you switch your fishing efforts to the outside of the bay?

"We start fishing on the ocean side around the first of June. Let me give you a bigger snapshot.

"I'll start down at Barnegat first, and fish it really hard with shrimp and spearing patterns. That's April and May. Right around mid-May, we get a huge in-flux of those big bunker in the Raritan Bay area. So, almost on a dime, I'll switch gears and start fishing up at Raritan."

A lot of guides fish only one area, but you're pretty mobile, right?

"I keep three slips throughout the year. I have a slip in Raritan Bay, I keep a slip in Barnegat Bay, and another in my main area in Point Pleasant."

So, you move and can always put people onto fish.

"That's the key to it. I go to the fish. And I use a bigger boat; I don't run off a trailer. I have a twenty-five-foot Parker with twins. I also do a lot of tuna on the fly, and I can easily go into the ocean with that boat. But, the Parker is a nice boat because it has a shallow draft so I can get into some areas that have shallow water. And I do a lot of trips. Last year I did two-hundred and twenty-five trips, which is a lot for a Northeast striper guide. So, I need to keep the boat in the water, not on a trailer."

When in the year do you start seeing the big fish?

"Let's talk about Raritan first. It's turned into a really world-class fishery. The majority of the fish we catch in Raritan Bay on the fly are over twenty pounds, and they go up to the high thirties and low forties. These are big fish."

What accounts for having such large stripers?

"First, you've got the Hudson River, which is the second largest wintering ground for spawning striped bass. What happens is really cool. By June, the big fish are coming out of the Hudson River following the bunker that are done spawning and coming out of the backwaters. At the same time, the tail end of the Chesapeake run of stripers is going up the beach. These are the really big fish: the thirty-, forty-, and fifty-pounders. For the past few years, this has all happened at the same time, and they've intersected right off my coastline.

"Second, there are a lot of bunker in those waters. There was a transition point where you could really see the change. In 2002, the State of New Jersey passed a law that restricted the commercial bunker-fishing boats from coming into our waters to get these bunker. Before 2002, massive amounts of bunker—picture schools the size of football fields containing two-pound bunker—would come into the bay and move along the surf. They'd be here for a couple of days, and we'd all go out and catch a couple of nice fish. Then the commercial-fishing boats would show up from all over the Northeast and

Dino's Bunker

eliminate these bunker. So, the state stopped that. It's made a tremendous difference and is helping New Jersey become a world-class fishery during the months of May and June.

"Sometime in the middle of May, when I get word that the bunker are in Raritan Bay, I'll move my boat up there. We'll start fishing the big pods of bunker for the larger bass. That's when we'll start throwing those bigger flies that I sent to you—a big Hollow Fly or Dino's Bunker Fly. Dino's Bunker Fly is my favorite because it does such a good job of matching the profile of a real bunker. And because it's tied with synthetics, it doesn't retain water and is easier for the average angler to cast."

What size of rod do you recommend for catching these big trophy stripers?

"I like using a ten-weight rod, and if there are really big fish around I'll go to an eleven-weight. But ninety percent of the time I prefer a good, sturdy ten-weight."

When do the bluefish show up?

"The blues are here the entire time the stripers are around. The blues enter New Jersey on the back of the mackerel run. As the mackerel come up the outer beaches, the blues are right on their tails and feeding on them. They'll then turn into the backwaters to feed. We'll get the razor bluefish, with the big heads and the long skinny bodies, around Mother's Day. So we'll be catching the blues in the exact same areas we're catching stripers."

Hollow Fly

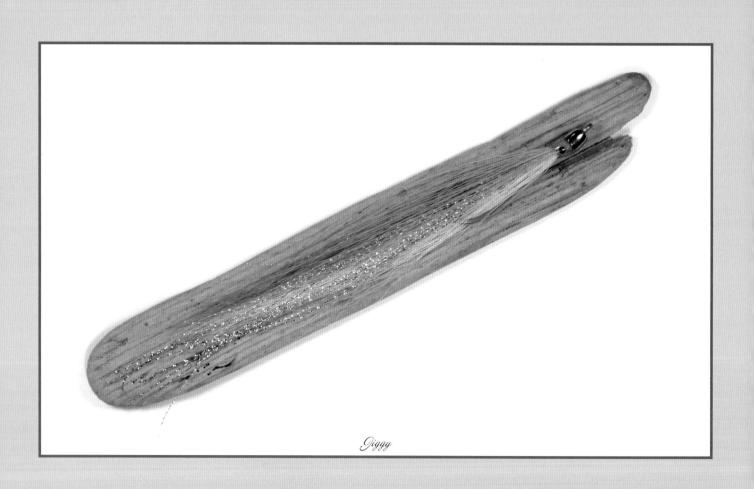

*Giggy*

Do you fish for the stripers throughout the entire summer?

"I'll keep on the stripers until the middle of July; it depends upon water temperature and how long the bass hang around. Once those big bass leave for the summer—the end of July, August, and September—I'm strictly offshore for tuna, albacore, bonito, skipjack and dolphin."

When in the fall do you begin fishing for stripers again?

"I pick back up on the stripers sometime around the end of September or the beginning of October. That's when the water chills and the mullet start coming out of the backwaters. The mullet trigger the beginning of the fall bass fishing."

How long is your fishing season?

"This year [2006-2007] I fished through the middle of January. December and the first two weeks of January were some of the best striper fishing we had both in terms of numbers and for the quality of the fly-fishing. We had a tremendous run of herring. I don't know if you saw it on the Internet, but some scientists took a satellite photo of what they said was the largest school of fish that they'd ever seen. These were the herring, and obviously there were stripers mixed in. They said the school was the size of Manhattan. It parked off the coast of New Jersey for about forty days, and the fishing was tremendous. And the beauty of that fishery is that the herring stay close to the surface, so there are a lot of bass crashing the surface and gannets dive-bombing; it's very visual and exciting. It also allows anglers to use floating and intermediate lines, which are a lot easier to cast than some of the heavier and more cumbersome lines we use in the spring."

What type of bait do you normally get in the fall?

"The typical fall and winter bait migration begins with mullet, then it turns to rainfish or bay anchovies. Next, we get the peanut bunker that are two to seven inches long. These are the bunker that were spawned that year; we get a very strong run of them for the tail end of October and most of the month of November. The rainfish are mixed in as well. Generally, the peanut bunker are right along the beach, and the bay anchovies will be a mile or two off the beach. We're still fishing on the outside; I don't fish the backcountry again until the following spring."

Aren't the seas a little rough for fishing during that time of the year?

"No, believe it or not, we tend to get high pressure and strong northwest winds. The way our beach is situated, this creates fairly flat seas out to about two miles. The wind is blowing off the beach, and the harder it blows, the flatter it gets. We can fish in twenty- to twenty-five mile an hour winds. We will get an occasional Nor'easter that will jam us up for two or three days in a row, but then it's back to the northwest and we're fishing again."

Do you get many guys who want to fish during that time year?

"It varies. But I do get a lot of clients at the end of the year who know the run will be spectacular. Some of them book once a week throughout December and early January."

You have a unique operation. Shore Catch Guide Service is actually several guides, and you offer beach as well as boat trips, don't you?

"Shore Catch Guide Service is kind of unique. In addition to offering boat trips, we also offer beach trips. I have four guides who are dedicated to taking anglers out on foot: in the surf, on jetties, and in the backwaters on the flats. And we have a total of six boats. As our business expands, I look for other qualified captains who are in the industry or want to get into the industry. But all of our clients book their trips through Shore Catch."

## Bob's Banger

**Hook:** Tiemco TMC911S, Eagle Claw 66SS, or Mustad 34011, size 4/0 or 2/0.
**Thread:** Any color of size D rod-wrapping thread.
**Wing:** White bucktail.
**Collar:** Red Estaz or Cactus Chenille.
**Body:** ½-inch or ¾-inch-diameter foam cylinder covered with silver prismatic tape.

## Dino's Bunker Fly

**Hook:** Tiemco TMC600SP, size 8/0.
**Thread:** Clear monofilament.
**Tail:** White Kinky Fiber.
**Body:** Yellow, pink, and olive Kinky Fiber.
**Eyes:** Large silver dome eyes.
**Head:** Epoxy.

## Dino's Marabou Minnow

**Hook:** Mustad Signature Series Big Game Light, size 2/0
**Thread:** Clear monofilament.
**Tail:** Long white marabou.
**Body:** Chartreuse bucktail.
**Eyes:** Large lead dumbbell eyes

## Geno's Baby Angel

**Hook:** Tiemco TMC600SP, size 3/0.
**Thread:** Clear monofilament.
**Tail (underbody):** Pearl green Angel Hair.
**Body (top):** Rainbow Angel Hair.
**Eyes:** Medium silver adhesive eyes.
**Gills:** Red Angel Hair.

## Half & Half

**Hook:** Mustad Signature Series Big Game Light, size 2/0.
**Thread:** Clear monofilament.
**Tail:** Four long, white saddle hackles.
**Body:** Red braid and white bucktail.
**Flash:** Silver or pearl Flashabou.
**Eyes:** Large lead dumbbell eyes.

## Popovics' Bucktail Deceiver

**Hook:** Tiemco TMC911S, size 2/0 to 4/0.
**Thread:** Danville's Flat Waxed Nylon. Select a color to match the head of the fly.
**Tail:** Long white bucktail tied in 360 degrees around the hook shank.
**Head:** Red bucktail tied 360 degrees around the hook shank.
**Eyes:** Large silver adhesive eyes.

## Popovics' Hollow Fleye

**Hook:** Tiemco TMC911S, size 2/0 or 4/0.
**Thread:** Danville's Flat Waxed Nylon, color to match the head of the fly.
**Tail:** Long yellow bucktail, tied 360 degrees around the hook shank.
**Body (head):** Chartreuse bucktail, tied 360 degrees around the hook shank.
**Eyes:** Large silver adhesive eyes

## Popovics' Jiggy Fleye

**Hook:** Tiemco 911S or an equivalent 3X-long hook, size 2/0.
**Head and weight:** Medium tungsten cone and .30-inch lead wire wrapped behind the head.
**Thread:** Clear monofilament
**Tail:** White bucktail.
**Body:** Olive bucktail, and pearl and purple Flashabou.
**Eyes:** Orange adhesive eyes.
**Note:** Coat the cone head and eyes with epoxy.

## Popovics' Surf Candy

**Hook:** Varivas 990 or an equivalent short-shank hook, size 2.
**Thread:** Clear monofilament.
**Belly:** White Unique Hair.
**Back:** Tan Unique Hair
**Eyes:** Silver adhesive eyes.
**Note:** Coat the front of the body around the hook shank with epoxy.

## Popovics' Ultra Shrimp

**Hook:** Regular saltwater hook, size 4.
**Thread:** Clear monofilament.
**Eyes:** Melted monofilament.
**Antennae:** White Ultra Hair with very short strands of pearl Flashabou.
**Legs:** Ginger hackle.
**Body:** Epoxy.
**Note:** This pattern was created by the legendary fly designer Bob Popovics.

## Lefty's Deceiver

**Hook:** Regular saltwater hook, sizes 4 to 2/0.
**Thread:** Black 6/0 (140 denier).
**Tail:** Saddle hackles and Krystal Flash.
**Wing and belly:** Bucktail.
**Topping:** Peacock herl.
**Gills:** Red Krystal Flash.
**Eyes:** Small adhesive eyes coasted with epoxy.
**Note:** Here we see a black Lefty's Deceiver, which is a favorite fly for fishing at night or in stained water. Of course you may tie this fly in your choice of favorite colors.

# TIER'S TUTORIAL: *Tying the Surf Candy*

If you're new to saltwater fly tying, then you'll eventually want to learn how to make the Surf Candy. This amazing design was created by New Jersey fly tying legend Bob Popovics. Although Bob isn't a guide, many professional captains do rely on his patterns. In addition to being a very good tier, he's also a hell of a nice guy; I always enjoy chatting with him, and he is always quick to share his knowledge. Here are the basic steps for making a Surf Candy. You may change the colors of the materials and tie the pattern in sizes to match the bait in your local waters.

In this example, I am tying a basic Sand Eel Surf Candy; this is one of my favorite flies. (And I *will* place this one in my fly box!)

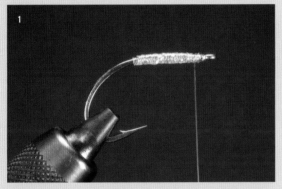

Start the clear monofilament thread on the hook shank. Tie a piece of tinsel or other flash material to the hook. Wrap the tinsel up the hook shank. Tie off and clip the excess tinsel.

Tie on a small amount of Ultra Hair or another synthetic material to form the belly of the fly.

Tie another color of Ultra Hair to the top of the hook to form the back of the fly. Sometimes Bob ties a piece of flash material on each side of the fly to imitate the flashy flanks of a baitfish, or you may tie on a few strands of your favorite flash material. Tie off and clip the thread.

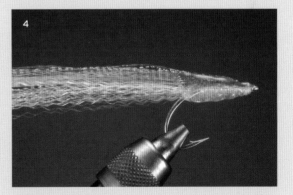

Coat the head of the fly with epoxy. Place the fly on a drying wheel until the epoxy hardens. Allow the epoxy to cure.

(tying steps continue on the next page)

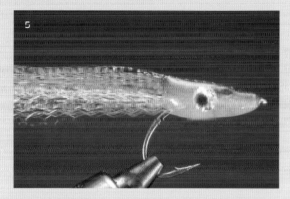

Place an adhesive eye on each side of the head. Apply a second coat of epoxy.

Clip the Ultra Hair to length. This example is an effective, durable imitation of a sand eel.

# The Big Apple
## with Capt. Joe Mustari

4

f you'd like to fish for striped bass in a more cosmopolitan setting, then why not test the waters around the Big Apple? Yes, I mean New York City. The mouth of the Hudson River, New York City Harbor, the East River, and the surrounding waters are a striped bass fisherman's paradise. Imagine fly-fishing with the Manhattan skyline and the Statue of Liberty as the backdrop. Incredible!

These are Capt. Joe Mustari's stomping grounds. He knows the watery ins and outs of northern New Jersey and New York City like the back of his hand, and can show you the best fishing. What he describes is a really unique fly-fishing experience for trophy bass.

"I'm from Staten Island; that's where I fish out of," Capt. Mustari said. "I was born and raised on Staten Island, and moved to New Jersey about eleven years ago.

"I fish out of Great Kills and Staten Island. I fish the entire Great Kills area, Raritan Bay, the Sandy Hook area, and all of lower New York Harbor. I also fish the East River all around Manhattan. That's all my turf. It's really unique because if people aren't

from town, they're pretty surprised. 'Oh,' they'll say, 'you're going to take me fishing around New York City?' And I'll say, 'Well, let's just give it a try. I think you'll probably be surprised.' And they are surprised. We'll be fishing right downtown from Wall Street, and we'll be catching nice fish."

It sounds like an amazing experience. I mean, a client can get to fish as well as take a scenic tour of the city.

"Absolutely. People are surprised, and they're very happy. They get the tour and the fishing. It's a really nice combination."

Do you ever get any resistance to what you're doing? I mean, some people must be skeptical.

"Sure. Five years ago, no one would want to come to New York Harbor and fly fish for striped bass, bluefish, and albacore. But there have been some articles written about it, and it's getting pretty popular."

How long is your fishing season?

"Our season is huge. That's another advantage. It's from April right through to Christmas. We have a big season."

Almost every Christmas I visit relatives in Philadelphia. A lot of people tell me that the fishing is actually good that time of year along the New Jersey

shore, but I really never believe them. So, you're telling me it would be worthwhile,

"You bet. The next time you're down, give me a call and we'll get together and fish. I think you'll love it."

Wait a minute. I've been to New York around Christmas time, and man, it's cold as hell!

"Yeah, it can be really cold, but the stripers don't care! You've got to pick your day. This past New Year's Day it was seventy degrees, and I think we caught a bass on every cast. It was ridiculous. We had a herring run that was just spectacular. There were no real big fish caught on flies—most of the fish were under ten pounds—but as far as action goes, it was fantastic. And that was on the last day of December! As long as the weather holds, it can really be something else."

Okay, you're fishing the mouth of the Hudson River. Are these primarily the Hudson River fish we all hear about?

"Well, I'll tell you, our area is really unique. I think we get both groups of fish. We get the Chesapeake Bay stripers as well as the Hudson River fish. We're right in the pathway where both strains of bass pass by. Sometimes, around Sandy Hook, those could all be Chesapeake fish. We're right on the bend where all of the fish start traveling east; they hit Long Island, and start traveling east."

Let's start with the early part the season. What's the first bait you get?

"In April, the bunker migration starts to happen. By the middle of May, we have our peak run of big

*Monster Bunker 11"*

stripers. You've heard of the flats in Maryland—the Susquehanna Flats. We have a very similar situation, except that it's not shallow water like those flats, but it's the same size fish. They come here and just keep feeding on the bunker. It's common to catch a fifteen- to twenty-pound fish almost every day."

Do you use big patterns that time of year?

"Yes, we use real big bunker imitations. That Monster Bunker is an excellent fly for fishing in May."

It's an awfully big fly, but it's made entirely out of synthetic materials so it must shed water and remain fairly easy to cast.

"Yes, it is very easy to cast. It's not a problem to throw it with an eight-weight rod. I like to use an eight-weight, but I like my customers to use a ten-weight because you never know when they might latch onto a big fish."

How deep is the water where you're fishing?

"Our bay averages anywhere from ten to thirty-five feet deep. When we're fishing thirty-five to forty feet deep, we'll be fishing the edge of the channels. This is really the entrance to New York Harbor. It's one of the biggest shipping ports in the world. There are dredged channels all through the bay where the big ships are going in and out all day long. A lot of times, the bunker and bass hang out along the edges of these channels. Sometimes we'll be fishing in thirty-five feet of water—sometimes even deeper."

What types of lines are you using to fish that deep?

"I use a three-hundred-fifty to five-hundred-grain sinking line. When I use a ten-weight, I'll be using a five-hundred-grain line and one of those big bunker flies. When I'm fishing in the shallows, I like a three-hundred or three-hundred-and-fifty-grain line."

How big are your tides?

"We have a six-foot tide; it's not nearly as big as it is on Cape Cod. But it's enough water that it can create some good, strong currents."

With all of the bunker in the water, do the bluefish show up early as well?

"The bluefish don't get the credit because there so many bass around, but the bluefish are just as good. Also in May, we get these big spawning weakfish. They're usually caught by accident; we really don't target them. But they can average ten to fifteen pounds, no problem. I'm not kidding. That's really a marvelous fish."

What's the next major run of bait?

"Right around the end of July or the first of August, the small juvenile bunker begin showing up. They can be anywhere from two to three inches long. By October, they're maybe five inches long. But you always have bunker in a variety of sizes."

I see you tie your bunker pattern in a variety of

sizes. You use one basic fly to match the entire life-cycle of the menhaden.

*Medium Bunker*

"Yes, that one basic pattern covers just about all the bases. I call it the 3-D Bunker because of the style in which it is tied. I've got to tell you that I give Bob Popovics credit for teaching me how to tie that fly. Bob really showed me how to tie that style, and I've been doing it that way for probably the past ten years. I tie a lot of my flies that way. I tie the 3-D Herring the same way."

And you really like olive-colored flies, don't you?

"I love olive, and I love chartreuse. I'm not too fancy with my colors."

What's the next big stage in your fishing season?

"Well, those big bass are definitely migrating fish. In April, you'll be catching fish that weigh less than ten pounds, then all of a sudden, you'll catch a twenty-pound fish. But the bigger bass will be here for only a while before they move on. When June comes, the bay heats up and those bigger bass will move off into the ocean around Sandy Hook and Breezy Point where the water is cooler. The bunker schools will also be out there, and as long as the bunker stay there, the bass will also hang around and you'll be able to catch them. They might stay there through June before moving on."

But do you have opportunities to fish for striped bass all summer?

"We have a lot of local fish that stay here all summer. They'll hang out in the rips and around the different structure There are a lot of rips, and I also fish around a lot of the islands. And there's a lot of bird action every day, so you'll always be able to pin-point the stripers. During mid-summer, it's a mix of bass and bluefish."

I understand that you do a lot of fishing in deep water, but do you ever have opportunities to fish top-water?

"I like fishing topwater in the morning when the water is calm and slick. I'll fish a Bob's Banger around structure. I'll fish it over a wreck or around rock piles. I really like fishing topwater when we have a mullet run. The fish always seem to be looking up when we have a mullet run, and that always seems to be the

best fly. This usually happens any time around the second or third week of September. It happens about the same time when the albacore show up."

Other than the big schools of bunker, as well as the mullet, what other types of bait do you have?

"We have a lot of different rain bait like bay or false anchovies. What I call the false anchovy is a bigger rain bait; it's probably about three inches long. Silversides, what we call spearing, are also very common. We also have varieties of shrimp, as well as crab hatches. I sent you a little popper. Instead of using a crab pattern, I use that little popper during a crab hatch. I just cast that fly in front of the fish and let it sit there. I actually made that popper for alba-core, then, one day I was getting frustrated watching the stripers eating all the small crabs, so I gave it try. And it worked!"

*Albie Popper*

You also sent a lovely little Surf Candy.
"I use that little Surf Candy when the rain bait is real small. It's an excellent imitation for matching that type of bait."

Do you ever try fishing with lighter tackle?

"Sometimes, during a summer evening when the water is real slick, I'll drop down to a six-weight rod, especially when they're feeding on shrimp or krill. The fish average five to six pounds apiece, so it's an awful lot of fun. Those fish hang out here all summer long."

I never think if your area as having flats or weeds.

*Rain Bait*

*Baby Bunker*

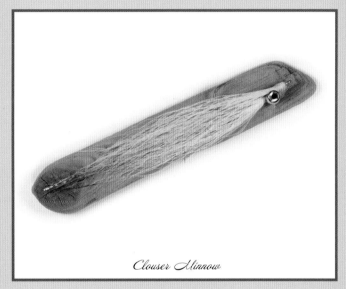

*Clouser Minnow*

*Deep Jiggy*

*Ultra Shrimp*

Where do the shrimp live?

"We have boggy areas and mussel beds and a lot of old piers. I do a lot of fishing around those old piers. These aren't structures you can stand on, you have to fish from the boat."

What type of bait do you have in the fall?

"In the fall we have butterfish, baby bunker, mullet, squid, and all the different rain fish. We have a wide variety of bait in the fall."

Before we were talking about all the wind in the New York City area. Can you still get out and fish on windy days?

"That's one of the great things about fishing in my area. We sometimes get a lot of wind, but I can always go into the Manhattan area, or the East River, and get out of all the weather."

A mutual friend, Henry Cowen, is the one that suggested that I interview Capt. Mustari. He said that I should ask Joe about the world record striper that was caught on his boat. "He won't bring it up," Henry warned. "He doesn't do a lot of bragging, so you'll have to ask him about it."

And sure enough, Capt. Mustari didn't mention the fish.

"Yes, I had a guy catch a world-record striper," Joe said with a laugh. "His name is Rick Fink, and he's from Staten Island. It was a twenty-pound-tippet class record. It was a forty-five-inch fish, and it weighed thirty-six pounds. He was using one of Henry Cowen's Magnum Bunker patterns. He caught that fish at the end of April

when all those big bunker and the big bass are here."

So, you're being serious: You catch some really big fish during the first part of the season.

"Oh yes, there are some really big fish around. Some of the guys who live-line the bunker catch some huge fish. Last year a guy caught a bass that weighed fifty-eight pounds."

That's an enormous striper, but can I catch something like that using flies? I mean, realistically, if I do everything right, and the moon and stars are lined up right, how big of a fish might I catch on a fly? Could I catch, say, a thirty-pounder?

"No, we don't get a lot of thirty-pound fish, but we catch a lot of fish in the twenties. This is an area where you can have a real legitimate chance of catching a twenty-pound bass on a fly."

*Wool Head Bunker*

All of a sudden I realized I was talking to a real expert on how to catch big striped bass on flies. I asked him what we need to know to catch a trophy fish.

"One of the important things is to use a big fly, especially around the bunker. You have to let the fly sink, and I like to move it slowly, and then speed it up, and then stop it. I stop it a lot during the retrieve. We do get a lot of refusals, and I've noticed that a lot of the big fish will turn around at the surface. When I start seeing that behavior, I'll stop the fly even more. What happens is that a lot of anglers just keep stripping the fly, and I'll tell them to just stop. Just let the fly hang in the water for two or three seconds. A lot of fish will eat it on the stop.

*Sand Eel*

*Half & Half*

"I definitely don't like a steady, tarpon-type retrieve. The bait is being chased, and it's very erratic. I like the retrieve to also be erratic. I don't like the retrieve to be consistent. This definitely works instead of a constant, steady retrieve."

Do you ever catch big stripers using poppers and other topwater flies?

"Sure, we've caught fish that weighed more than twenty pounds on poppers during the mullet run.

"What it all boils down to," Capt. Joe concluded, "is that you've just got to be persistent. And you've got to believe."

### Monster 3D Bunker Fly

**Hook:** Short-shank, size 7/0.
**Thread:** Clear monofilament.
**Body:** White, yellow and olive Kinky Fiber, and gold, silver, and pearl Polar Flash. Tie on the Kinky Fiber using the hi-tie method, and then blend the fibers using a comb.
**Gills:** Pink Angel Hair.
**Eyes:** Extra-large adhesive eyes.
**Note:** To create a fly of this size, which measures 12 inches long, Capt. Mustari ties the body in five stages up the hook shank. He uses a black permanent marker to add the spot on the head.

### Medium 3D Bunker Fly

**Hook:** Short-shank, size 5/0.
**Thread:** Clear monofilament.
**Body:** White, yellow and olive Kinky Fiber, and gold, silver, and pearl Polar Flash. Tie on the Kinky Fiber using the hi-tie method, and then blend the fibers using a comb.
**Gills:** Pink Angel Hair.
**Eyes:** Large silver dome eyes.
**Note:** This is the middleweight in Capt. Mustari's series of 3D Bunker Flies. It is about 8 inches long.

### Peanut 3D Bunker Fly

**Hook:** Short-shank, size 5/0.
**Thread:** Clear monofilament.
**Body:** White, yellow and olive Kinky Fiber, and gold, silver, and pearl Polar Flash. Tie on the

Kinky Fiber using the hi-tie method, and then blend the fibers using a comb.
**Gills:** Pink Angel Hair.
**Eyes:** Medium silver dome eyes.

### Baby 3D Bunker

**Hook:** Regular length, sizes 2 and 1.
**Thread:** Clear monofilament.
**Body:** White and olive Poly Bear.
**Note:** This is the baby of the group. It measures only about 2 inches long.

### Clouser Deep Minnow

**Hook:** Mustad Signature C70S, size 2/0.
**Thread:** Clear monofilament.
**Eyes:** Medium dumbbell.
**Tail:** White and chartreuse bucktail with strands of silver and gold Flashtail or Flashabou.
**Note:** Yes, this is one of the most famous of all striped bass patterns dressed in the most common colors. If you don't have a chartreuse-and-white Clouser Minnow in your fly box, then you're not a serious striped bass fisherman.

### Half & Half

**Hook:** Regular saltwater hook, size 2/0 to 4/0.
**Thread:** Clear monofilament.
**Eyes:** Large dumbbell.
**Tail:** White saddle hackles with strands of narrow gold Flashabou.
**Belly:** White bucktail.
**Back:** Pink and olive bucktail.
**Note:** One of the problems in researching this book is that some of the captains sent some of the same flies. I was in no position to argue with any of these folks; after all, we are being given the privilege to have a peek inside their fly boxes. So, you may find the Half & Half listed elsewhere in this book. What we should take away from this is that the Half & Half is a professional go-to fly. Tie it, use it, and you too will catch more stripers. Also, carefully examine any of the same flies you find sprinkled throughout this book; there are only one or two that are repeated. See how different experienced guides approach tying the same fly;

sometimes this is just as important as being given an entirely new recipe.

### Sand Eel Fly

**Hook:** Long-shank saltwater hook, size 2.
**Thread:** Clear monofilament.
**Eyes:** Medium dumbbell.
**Tail:** White and olive FisHair with strands of Polar Flash or narrow pearl Flasbou.

### Wool Head Bunker

**Hook:** Regular saltwater hook, size 2/0.
**Thread:** Clear monofilament.
**Tail:** White and olive Kinky Fiber, and gold and pearl Polar Flash.
**Head:** White wool. Color the top of the head with an olive permanent marker.
**Eyes:** Medium pearl dome eyes glued to the sides of the head.

### Rain Bait Surf Candy

**Hook:** Short-shank saltwater hook, sizes 6 to 1/0.
**Thread:** Clear monofilament.
**Body:** White and tan craft fur, and pearl Bill's Bodi Braid wrapped on the hook shank. There are also some strands of extra-fine pearl Flashabou in the tail of the fly.
**Eyes:** Small or extra-small silver adhesive eyes.
**Head:** Epoxy.
**Note:** Bob Popovics' Surf Candy is the quintessential striped bass pattern. You'll find different examples of this fly throughout the book. See how these expert guides use this basic design to create patterns to meet their local fishing conditions.

### Deep Jiggy

**Hook:** 3X-long saltwater hook, size 3/0.
**Head:** Large tungsten cone with adhesive eyes.

**Thread:** Clear monofilament.
**Tail:** Chartreuse and white bucktail with strands of gold and silver Flashabou.
**Note:** Wrap lead wire on the hook shank behind the cone to add additional weight to the head of the fly.

### Albie Popper

**Hook:** Regular saltwater hook, size 2.
**Thread:** Clear monofilament.
**Tail:** Tan and white craft fur.
**Body:** Small Live Body foam popper covered with E-Z Body tubing.
**Eyes:** Small or medium adhesive eyes.
**Note:** Coat the entire body with Plasti-Dip, Softex, or a similar product.

### Worm or Krill Fly

**Hook:** Regular saltwater hook, size 4 or 2.
**Thread:** Chartreuse 6/0 (140 denier).
**Eyes:** Small lead dumbbell.
**Tail:** Chartreuse bucktail and an orange grizzly Zonker strip.
**Back:** A tuft of olive rabbit hair.
**Body:** The tying thread.

*Peanut Bunker*

*Worm Fly*

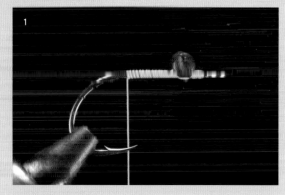

Start the thread on the hook, and tie on the small dumbbell.

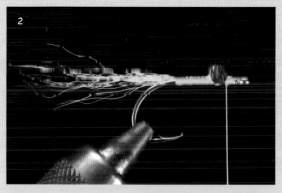

Tie on a small amount of chartreuse bucktail to form the tail of the fly; attach the material to the hook in front of the dumbbell. Wrap the thread down the hook, binding the bucktail to the shank. Wrap the thread back to the hook eye.

Poke a hole in an orange Zonker strip. Thread the needle through the hole. Tie down the front end of the strip. Clip the excess.

Tie a small tuft of olive rabbit fur to the top of the fly.

Tie off and clip the thread. Coat the thread wraps with cement.

# 5

## Capt. Joe Blados
## Invents the Crease Fly

*I* can't imagine a serious striped bass fisherman who hasn't used a Crease Fly. Hell, fly anglers are using Crease Flies to catch all kinds of fish. The Crease Fly is a very simple fly to make, and a delight to use. I'll show you how to make the Crease Fly at the end of this chapter, but for right now, let me tell you about Capt. Joe Blados.

As you will learn, Capt. Joe is a native of Long Island, New York. He grew up on the water, and spends most of the summer guiding anglers to the area's great fishing for striped bass, bluefish, albacore, and other favorite game fish. Capt. Blados is also the inventor of the Crease Fly. Lately, because of his fa-

mous pattern, he's become somewhat of a modern legend. I really don't think he would like me saying that, he seems far too modest, but it's the truth. I think it would also be fair to say that the Crease Fly is the most popular topwater fly. Yes, there are all sorts of popular poppers, but let's face it, they are all a variation on the same theme. Joe, however, came up with an entirely new way to create a topwater fly. It's quick and easy to make, very light to cast, and attracts—but does not spook—the fish. Once you get the hang of the construction technique, you'll be able to make a box full of Crease Flies in just a couple of evenings; you probably won't be able to do that making standard poppers.

I caught up with Capt. Blados around the first of December. He had enjoyed a busy year of productive fishing, and things were beginning to slow down a bit. The weather had changed for a few days, and he had time for our interview.

"We should be in the middle of good fishing," he said, "but last week we had a Nor'easter, and I tell you what: It raised hell and put everything down into deeper water."

Capt. Blados lives on the far northern tip of Long Island. He described his home waters and the advantage they give him for enjoying some quiet yet very worthwhile fishing.

"I'm on the north fork of Long Island, all the way on the east end. There are two points to Long Island. If you look at Long Island on a map, it looks like a fish tail. You have Montauk on one point, which is really good fishing, but there's a lot of pressure and competition over there. Sometimes it's a damn zoo. It's more laid back where I am, and the fishing is just as good. As a matter of fact, a lot of those guys were over here last week because the albies were still here and they'd lost theirs over on that side of the island. It happens that way every year, but they'll eventually get the big bass run with the herring, which we don't get over here. It's a tradeoff. I occasionally go over to Montauk, but my thing is to have a good day with less stress. You don't need a hundred boats cutting you off; it's too crowded for what I like to do. I love taking kids and women out—you know, 'newbies.' So I like to avoid all the hairy competition and just have a nice day and catch fish."

You've lived and worked on the water almost all your life, haven't you?

"I started as a commercial fisherman working with my grandfather. When you grew up out here, you were either a commercial fisherman or a farmer.

Those were the predominant industries out here years ago. Half of my family were commercial fishermen, so I dragged my tail over on the boats all the time. But the handwriting was on the wall, and commercial fishing is almost obsolete out here; it's hard to make a living, and you have to have a second income to pull through. But, I started out as a commercial fisherman, and I always took a spinning rod out on the boat."

Now we're getting to the really interesting part of the story: how Joe discovered fly-fishing.

"We were fishing the back side of Gardner's Island for porgies, which is one of the best flats in the world for sight fishing to striped bass. We were fishing for bass before anyone else was there. You'd set the nets, and there was a long time before you'd check them, and I'd fish for bass with the spinning rod. After a while there wasn't any challenge to using the spinning rod, so that's when I said I wanted to do something a little more interesting. So, I thought I would try fly-fishing."

Were there any guys fly-fishing for striped bass at that time?

"Yes there were, but fly-fishing was kind of low keyed back then. There wasn't anybody here to show you how to do it. I didn't know anybody who fly-fished. It was a matter of trial and error, and more error than anything! I mean, you spent more money buying stuff that was useless because most of the tackle was geared toward trout fishermen. But that's how you learn, man. I remember catching my first bluefish on a fly rod. You never forget something like that."

What kind of patterns were you using?

"We were using Deceiver-type patterns, simple stuff like that. But that's the other thing: I always wanted to get into the creative end of it. Between painting motorcycles and doing artwork, I wanted to be creative with my fly-fishing. Fly tying is pretty much in the same category. It is an art.

"My thing was realism. I was into realistic looking things more than patterns that didn't look like anything living in saltwater. That doesn't mean that fish won't eat those unrealistic patterns. I mean, come on, chartreuse? There aren't too many things running around in the water that are chartreuse, but it's one of

the best colors you can use. I was making wooden plugs and all kinds of things, but this is how you start out."

It turns out that it was in an effort to create a fly with the tall profile of a baitfish that Joe hit on the idea for the Crease Fly.

"We have an abundance of peanut bunker out here in the fall. They have a body that is a totally different shape from any of the flies that were around. To create flies with that basic shape, I'd hollow out Live Body cylinders I bought from the Dale Clemens catalog. I'd then squeeze them together and glue them to the hook shanks. That gave you the basic profile of a peanut bunker. The key was to get the tall profile, and make it basically 'match the hatch.'

"Well, my little bunker pattern was working, but the next thing you know my wife is hollering at me that the house if full of foam dust. That's when I came up with the idea to use sheet foam. It was so much simpler to make it that way, and that's how I came up with the Crease Fly."

Okay, Joe had created a great new fly. Unfortunately, none of us knew about it. Fortunately, he met Bob Popovics, who saw to it that we all learned about the Crease Fly.

"I met Bob Popovics years ago at the fishing show in Suffern, New York. Bobby was just getting started, and I was getting started. That was the big show back then; there really weren't any fly-fishing shows. The Suffern show was just a big sporting event. That was the first time I met Bob. God, that's going back. I can't tell you how long ago that was, but it's at least twenty-five years. Well, I gave him some Crease Flies, and that's how we struck up a relationship.

"I didn't really didn't get into publicizing the Crease Fly, but Bob got me involved with Umpqua Feather Merchants. I had submitted the pattern to Umpqua before, but Bobby helped it get noticed. They added it to their catalog of flies, and it grew from there."

One of the advantages of the Crease Fly is that it makes just a slight gurgling or churning noise on the surface of the water. It attracts the fish, it doesn't spook them. And, you can use a Crease Fly with different lines to meet different fishing situations.

"The Crease Fly really isn't a popper. You can use

it with a floating line, an intermediate line, or a sinking line. With a floating line, I can use a Crease Fly on the flats and it can be subtle enough and not freak out every goddamned fish. If you use Bob's Banger on the flats, forget it; the fish are so weary as it is—in two feet of water—that if you make too much noise you'll freak 'em out. The fish can humble you because nothing works all the time, but there are times when I can't get them on Clousers or other flies, but the Crease Fly will get them. And it's really fun to watch them get aggressive on Crease Flies in two feet of water."

You're absolutely right about making too much noise, I said. I fish in a couple of local estuaries, and I've noticed that if you make too much noise, you'll spook the fish.

"That's just it. There are times when you want to use a loud fly, but there are also times when you need a pattern that is more subtle. And if you use a sinking line, it acts like a totally different fly."

Yes, the Crease Fly pushes a lot of water under the surface which makes it easy for the fish to find.

"Well, that's part of it, but the Crease Fly also has a shake and wobble to it, which is a great action. You were talking about estuaries. Well, in early spring, before the flats really take off—I'm talking about April—a lot of fish come up into the estuaries because this is the first place the water warms up and this is the first place you get a food source, whether it's grass shrimp, alewives, or early bunker, which are really humongous because they're about a foot long. A lot of the estuaries are dredged channels and mosquito-ditch type deals where they drop off to about twelve feet from the bank. I cast parallel to the bank using a sinking line and a longer leader—maybe nine feet long, which is rare with a sinking line. I let the belly of the line go down. I then give the line three or four aggressive strips, which pulls the fly under the water. I then stop retrieving, and the fly flutters up. That's usually when you'll get a hit; when the fly rises to the surface. You have to pay attention and be quick on setting the hook. If you're not fast, the fish will strike the fly and spit it out."

Do you see many guys using Crease Flies with sinking lines?

"Nick Curcione was one of the first. And so does Dan Blanton, at least according to his Web site. But Nick was fishing around the oil rigs down in Louisiana and around the wrecks off California, and he was using the Crease Fly with a sinking line. It's a very effective technique."

Tell me about making the Crease Fly. Obviously the main part of the body is closed-cell sheet foam. What type of foil do you use for the skin?

"Several companies make the foil. All it is, is a transfer craft foil. If you place it on any sticky surface, it will release itself off the cellophane backing. The stuff adds virtually no weight to a fly, and it's waterproof. You really don't have to coat the fly with epoxy if you don't want to. I like the silver foil because almost all of the bait we have out here has some silver, and I think the silver flash is a triggering mechanism. My wife retired from her job, and now all she does is make Crease Fly kits. We sell them wholesale to fly shops."

How did you get into guiding?

"When I got out of the military, I was a bad-ass biker for about twenty years. We were building bikes inside the house here, and spray painting them. My biggest thing was doing the airbrush work; I loved messing around with the airbrush. When I got married, I kind of pulled away from the bikes. With that and with all the accidents you have bar hopping at night—the bones don't heal as well when you get older—it was time to hang it up, so I sold the choppers and bought my first Maverick flats skiff. That's when I started guiding. Now, come May or June, I'm fishing flat out. And sight fishing is the only bloody kind of fishing that there is. It's such a challenge. Just because you see a hundred fish a day doesn't mean you're going to catch them. Your cast has to be right on the money two feet in front of that fish's nose. If the fly comes straight at the fish, it knows there's no such thing as kamikaze bait, and it won't strike that damn fly. These fish can be very fussy."

When does your fishing season begin?

"I start fishing the last week of April in the estuaries, and then start on the flats the beginning of May and into June. My main flats are in Great Peconic Bay and Little Peconic Bay. There are many miles of flats; so many they haven't all been explored. It's really nice because even if you have a windy day, you can get out of the wind by going to the leeward side of an island. But like all flats fishing, the key is to have the

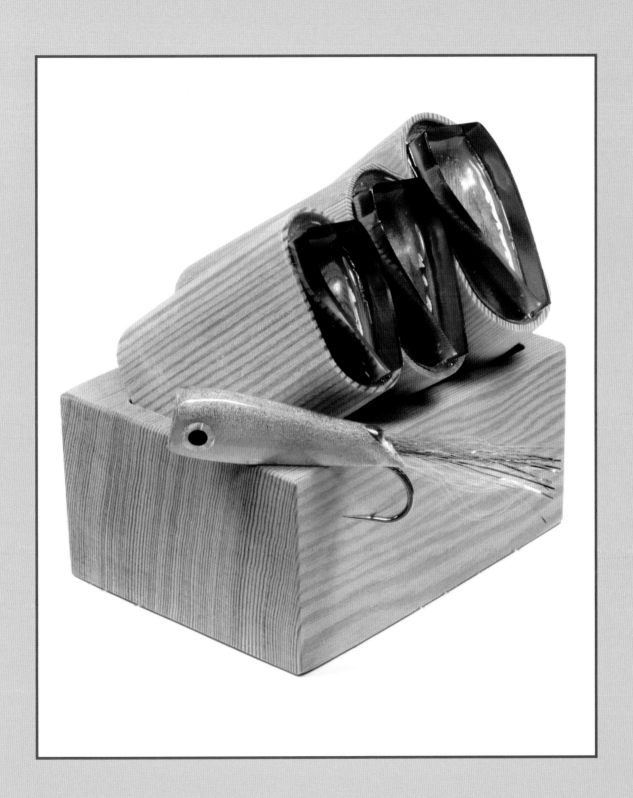

sun. If you have sun, you have it made because you'll see a lot of fish."

In addition to chartreuse, what other colors of flies do you like?

"The funny thing is that within the last few years, I swear to God, I thought all the bass were gay. I've been fishing these pink flies that don't look like anything in the water. You've got sand eels all around the boat, and you put that pink fly on, and a bass will go a mile out of its way to hit it. But put on a sand eel pattern, and the fish won't care. I found it out the hard way, but in the last two years we've almost doubled our catch just by using pink flies. Sure, there are cinder worms that you might say are sort of pink, and shrimp, but they don't turn pink until they're cooked. But pink has been deadly: The fish flare their gills and really hit them."

How do you work the flats with the changing tides? Do the tides complicate the fishing?

"We have about a four foot tide in the bay, so it's pretty mild. But you'll change positions depending upon the tides. Some flats are great when the tide is rising; others are better when the tide is falling. If you can find a current crossing a flat or bar, those fish love that. And the more the water that is moving, the better they like it.

"We have a peninsula on one island where there's almost always about a three-knot current that flows over this bar. Thirty-pound fish will lay right against the shoreline. I've seen spin-rodders go in there and try everything in the boat and catch nothing. Believe it or not, but *Fly Tyer* author Morgan Lyle is about the only guy who's caught one of those fish. He was using a little grass-shrimp pattern, and one of those fish did eat it. So, it just goes to show that you don't always need a big fly to catch a big fish!"

When does your season start to slow down?

"I keep fishing until the end of October, but it depends on the weather. October is windy, and November is cold and windy. When you're using a flats boat—and I love that Maverick—there are limitations. It gets to a point where it's not fun anymore. But if it's a good day, and there are fish in the area, I'll be out on the water."

## Crease Fly

**Hook:** Long-shank saltwater hook, sizes 2 to 3/0.

**Thread:** White 3/0 (280 denier).

**Tail:** Bucktail, Flashabou, and Krystal flash, in your choice of colors.

**Body:** Adhesive-back closed-cell craft foam covered with your choice of craft foil, coated with epoxy.

**Eyes:** Large adhesive eyes.

**Note:** From time to time you'll see tiers using slightly different methods to create Crease Flies. This is the recipe we'll use to make the Crease Fly in the accompanying photographs. It's simple, and the flies are very effective. You'll find the foam and sheet foil in craft stores. You'll also find the foam, and probably the foil, in the crafts section of your local discount retailer. (That's editorial shorthand for Wal-Mart.) The object of this lesson is to keep it cheap and have fun, and be creative.

If you want to take it up a notch and get really serious, consider using the Crease Fly body cutters offered by River Roads Creations. The folks at River Roads, which offers an entire family of fly tying wing and body cutters, worked with Capt. Joe Blados to design a set of cutters designed for punching out foam Crease Fly bodies. These high-quality tools are a hoot to use, and they'll help give your Crease Flies a polished, professional look. Check out the Capt. Joe Blados' Crease Fly Popper Cutters at www.riverroadcreations.com.

Remove the paper backing from the foam. Place the foil on the adhesive. You may now punch out the body using a Capt. Joe Blados' Crease Fly Popper Cutter (that's what I did here), or you may fold the foam in half and use your scissors to cut out the body. Note the little notch at the narrow end of the body: I clipped that using scissors. That notch will make it easier to fold the foam body around the hook shank.

Start the thread on the hook. Tie on one or two small amounts of bucktail in your favorite colors, and add a few strands of flash material. Tie the butt ends of the bucktail along the hook shank; this forms a base for gluing the foam body to the fly. Tie off and clip the thread.

Coat the thread wraps with superglue. Fold the foam body on the hook. Pinch the body together until the glue dries; this should take only about 30 seconds.

Place an adhesive eye on each side of the fly. You may use permanent markers to color the back of the fly and add other markings.

Coat the body with epoxy. Be sure to cover the edges of the foil at the mouth and along the bottom of the body to increase the durability of the fly. Place your Crease Fly on a drying wheel until the epoxy hardens.

# 6

## Rhode Island's
## Capt. Ray Stachelek

*M*oving up the Striper Coast, we next come to Rhode Island. These are the stomping grounds of Capt. Ray Stachelek, a retired teacher turned full-time guide. Capt. Ray also writes about his fishing and tying experiences, and lectures at fly-fishing clubs and shows throughout the Northeast. He's a very personable fellow who is always eager to share what he knows.

Capt. Ray has strong opinions about fly design based on years of hard fishing. He's a very inventive tier, and is always looking for new ways to create fresh patterns to catch striped bass, bluefish, false albacore, tuna, and the other species of game fish that inhabit Rhode Island's waters throughout the summer. Ray started tying flies when he was very young; this was years before there were clubs and the wide variety of instructional materials that help new tiers get on the fast track to success. As it turns out, however, he was fortunate to meet several fellows who showed him how to make good fish-catching flies.

"I started tying flies when I was eleven or twelve years old. I grew up in Providence, and then we moved to the shore. I'm fifty-nine years old now, and back then there were no books or anyplace to go and get good information. But, there were a lot of guys in my area who did tie flies. Some of them have become kind of famous, like Al Brewster; he became a really well known tier. Al was a neighbor who lived about a quarter of a mile away. It's kind of funny, but his grand kids came through my classes when I became a teacher. J. Edson Leonard was another famous tier and author who lived in my area. So there was a bunch of people in that area who fished and compared notes."

Did you start with tying saltwater flies?

"No I didn't. I started tying freshwater flies, and got into saltwater fishing when we moved to the shore. There was a bait shop in the area that had a small section of tying materials. We had small bluefish that weighed one or two pounds apiece; they were yearlings. We called them skipjacks when I was a kid. I caught them using a Fenwick freshwater bass fly rod; I was only about twelve years old. But guys were tying flies and catching those fish long before it became popularized in print.

"Back then, we adapted salmon and bass flies to our needs. We made adjustments, like using 6X-long hooks, and we didn't tie anything on the back end of the hook, everything was tied close to the hook eye and had shoulders to imitate gills. I don't think anything was tied closer to the end of the hook shank until Lefty started tying his Deceivers. And then they started using shorter saltwater hooks."

You were a technology teacher. Were you able to bring any of your fishing experiences into the classroom as a way to motivate the kids?

"Yes, I taught in middle school. It was fun because I'd show kids in woodworking class how to turn a plug. They got a big kick out of it, to make something they could actually use. I'm retired now, and I've been guiding about ten years."

When does the season for striped bass begin in Rhode Island?

"The spinning season for stripers can actually go year around. We have some holdover fish. There's a power plant in Rhode Island and several streams that

*Green Envy*

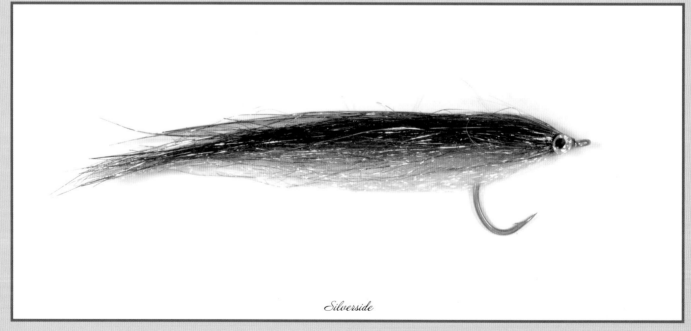

*Silverside*

hold fish all winter. Some of the stories go back to catching stripers through the ice in brackish water. When we were kids, we knew that when trout season opened—that was the second Saturday in April—that there were some stripers around. We didn't tell anybody, but we caught some stripers in a few of the estuaries at the end of March. We had a secret society doing this, but then other guys found out about it."

When does the fly-fishing season kick off?

"I start getting the boat ready sometime during the last two weeks of April, and some small schoolie bass show up in Narragansett Bay. A second slug of fish come into Narragansett Bay around May fourteenth; it's almost like clockwork. These fish weigh eight to twelve pounds apiece. The migrations of all these fish are triggered by the runs of bait. The first schoolies come in following spearing and silversides that are heading into the estuaries. The second influx of bass occurs when herring and other anadromous fish come in; those bigger fish are following the larger bait. The final push of bass, which can weigh up to thirty pounds apiece, are following the squid; this is late May and June. The squid are mostly along the coast in the colder water, but we do get some squid in Narragansett Bay."

You have the bay, estuaries, and then the ocean side—including Block Island—to fish. With so many possibilities, how do you decide where to start?

"To fish for stripers, you have to follow the migrations of the bait and the bass. You fish them in stages. You'll first look for the stripers in the estuaries in the warmer water where the bait gathers. I look in the smaller bays and estuaries that are shallower and contain shrimp and mummichogs. These are places that attract the first smaller fish. The second slug of larger fish go into the same bays and estuaries, but they head into the mouths of the rivers and streams following the anadromous bait. There's also a lot of good open-water fishing with that second run of fish that are chasing Atlantic herring."

What kind of tackle do you use?

"We use sinking lines when we fish from the boat. In the early part of the season, flies with olive and white do a good job of imitating the mummichogs. Shrimp patterns also work. But in the spring, I think you can be less concerned with using an exact imitation because the water is tinted; this is when an angler should be more concerned with the size and movement of the fly through the water. I don't think exact appearance is important until the lack of waves and current give the fish a better chance to get close to the fly and really study it."

How deep are you fishing?

"In the bay, the fishing is between eighteen and twenty feet deep; fishing any deeper with flies becomes less effective. On the ocean side in the autumn, you fish deeper in places, but you hope baitfish will be pushed toward the surface to get the stripers closer."

Block Island is legendary for its striped bass fishing. I've never fished there. What's it like, and when do you fish there?

"Block Island is a good spot. The cliffs are beautiful, but it's deep water. You're fishing from thirty-five to forty feet of water. The prime time is from June until the fall, but the water gets warm and the fish lay closer to the bottom. Wire and lead-core lines—trolling methods—seem to work best. And free-bailing with live eels also works. June, however, when the squid are around North Rip, is a good time to fish with flies. There's also some pretty good bonito and false albacore fishing on some of the flats. But other than that you have to spend a lot of time out there or live there to hit it right.

"When it comes to fly-fishing, I think there are three places you have to go at least once in your life: Block Island, Montauk, and Gay Head on Martha's Vineyard. They may not always fish the best, but they're like the Holy Grail of fly-fishing for ocean going striped bass."

So, you stay mobile and moving around Narragansett Bay and on the oceanside throughout the season.

"Yes, the first third of the fishing season occurs around the mid-bay islands. The second third is anywhere from Hope to Block Island, south to the bridges at Newport. After that, the fish move along the shore for the fall migration."

Do you use the same types of flies to fish these different areas?

"I noticed that at times, in deeper water, the flies I

was using weren't as effective when the fish moved into different zones. So I change flies to match the depth of the water, but I guess most guides do that."

Let's talk about your flies. The Stealth Wing Streamer is an unusual pattern.

*Stealth Wing*

"I got the idea for the Stealth Wing Streamer from an old steelhead type of fly that had a double hook. I played around with the idea of locking together two hooks so they wouldn't twist. The eyes are the key: I place the hooks back to back with the eyes touching, and wrap the shanks with monofilament thread. I then coat the mono with epoxy. This gives the fly a dipping action, and the two hooks create a flat profile that is perfect for tying on the wing. It's also fairly weedless: You can actually let the fly rest on the bottom and it won't snag. It's a very neat rig for flats fishing.

"By the way, most anglers don't realize it, but how you finish the thread head is very important on any fly you tie. The end of the wire that loops back to form the hook eye has a small burr that can chafe the tippet. This, of course, weakens the tippet, and is a great way to lose a good fish. I solve this by wrapping the thread so that the head covers the end of the wire and that burr. Another thing you can do is thread any flash material through the hook eye to cover the end of the wire."

Your Rabbit Eel is another original pattern of yours.

*Rabbit Eel*

"The Rabbit Eel contains two separate pieces of E-Z Body tubing, which is kind of unusual. What's neat is that the rabbit fur coming out of the front piece of tubing simulates gills. I also wrap the hook shank with large chenille to create an underbody that keeps the E-Z Body tubing round. You can also slip a cone on the hook before tying the fly to add weight. I use these to fish in places like Cape Cod Canal where you have a current and need a weighted fly to get down."

*Ultra Bright Rattle Squid*

I love your Ultra Bright Rattle Squid. This fly must have a lot of action in the water.

"Squid are very important to our fishing. I tie dif-

*Herring*

ferent varieties of squid flies When I started tying the
Ultra Bright Rattle Squid, I made it in pink. But then
I started really examining squid and found that they
sometimes get infuriated and turn pink, but there are
other times when they're brown and purple—a mot-
tled or camouflage scheme.

"We get big squid action from Newport Shores to
Westerly. That's my secret to catching big fish. Everybody thinks that squid are seasonal and they'll fish
squid patterns in the spring, but there are times where
you have fast-moving water that is thirty-five to forty
feet deep, and the fish will push the squid up on these
subsurface reefs that are only five or six feet deep, and
along some of the rock outcroppings. Sometimes the
squid will actually leap out of the water."

Capt. Ray pointed out that the flies and fishing
tactics that work along one section of the Striper
Coast might not be effective in another area. You
have to spend time on the water and learn the local
fishing conditions.

"Every saltwater place has a rhythm—Rhode Island, Cape Cod, or whatever. I finally discovered the
answer to catching big fish in Rhode Island. First, I
had to retire so I could fish every day and chase the
big stripers! Yeah, I'm being funny, but now I have
the time to fish and observe the stripers when there
are fewer boats on the water. When I was teaching, I
was doing a lot of guiding on weekends; I had almost
no free time for my own recreational fishing. Now, I
can go out and find the conditions I like, and I can
catch bigger fish."

You tie a nice anchovy imitation. When do you
use this pattern?

"The Bay Anchovy is a fall pattern. Sometimes
we fish all the way into December; I just put the boat
away. [I conducted this interview with Capt. Stachelek
a couple of weeks before Christmas.] It all depends
on the temperatures. This year guys are still fishing
because the temperature is still around forty-eight
degrees. I pulled the boat out of the water because
you have to winterize it before the first snowstorm,
but we still fish from shore. Another option is to have
a small boat that you can stow in the garage and take
out on calm days."

When do you use the Juvie Menhaden?

"The Juvie Menhaden is a late summer and fall

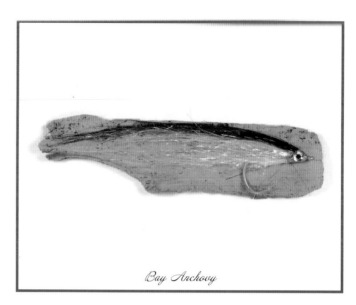

Bay Anchovy

Juvie Menhaden

pattern. It represents the small young-of-the-year
menhaden."

Angel Hair is a great material for tying effective
saltwater flies. You use it on a lot of your patterns.

"I started tying the Angel Hair series about ten
years ago. I got a bunch of material from the manufac-
turer, but about three years later I started seeing a lot
of similar materials on the market. No one accepted it
right away because they couldn't figure out how to use
it to make patterns with larger profiles. But I worked
on it and found out how to use Angel Hair."

Sardines are common to many waters. I bet your
sardine imitation would work in a lot of places.

"That Sardine is another fall pattern, but it also
works well around Florida. We really don't have a lot

*Sardine*

*Herring*

of sardines, but it's such a close imitation of a silver side that you can use it and catch fish."

You like to use a mixture of colors on your flies. I think this gives them a very realistic appearance in the water.

"I tie a lot of flies with all different colors to create contrast. I tie a Clouser Minnow with all Ultra Hair. When people look at it they say there are only three steps, but no there aren't; there are actually six or seven subtle changes of Ultra Hair. The more subtle changes you make, the more prismatic a fly becomes. If you look at the scales of a baitfish, no matter how the light reflects off them, they constantly change colors. Using various colors to mimic this prismatic effect is very important."

Tell me about your Atlantic Herring.

"The Atlantic Herring is a good fly for the late spring and summer when the real herring are around. But it's kind of a generic pattern that can be used anytime to represent butterfish and other species. That pattern got developed because of the way the Angel Hair flutters as the fly sinks through the water. I started tying bucktail on the belly and back of the fly to build a cage on the fly so that it retains its shape when it sinks."

Capt. Ray Stachelek is an excellent instructor and inventive fly tier. You won't go wrong adding his patterns to your fly box.

### Angel Hair Silverside

**Hook:** Regular saltwater hook, size 2.
**Thread:** Clear monofilament.
**Body:** Pearl, olive, and dark green Angel Hair.
**Eyes:** Small silver dome eyes.

### Angel Hair Juvie Menhaden

**Hook:** Regular saltwater hook, size 2.
**Thread:** Clear monofilament.
**Body:** Pearl and dark green Angel Hair.
**Eyes:** Small silver dome eyes.
**Note:** Use a black permanent marker to color the spot on the side of the body.

### Angel Hair Bay Anchovy

**Hook:** Regular saltwater hook, size 4.
**Thread:** Clear monofilament.
**Body:** Pearl, brown, and dark blue Angel Hair.
**Eyes:** Small silver dome eyes.

### Angel Hair Sardine

**Hook:** Regular saltwater hook, size 2.
**Thread:** Clear monomfilament.
**Body:** Pearl, olive, and dark green Angel Hair.
**Eyes:** Medium silver dome eyes.

### Rabbit Eel

**Hook:** Long-shank saltwater hook, size 4 or 2.
**Weight:** Cone bead.
**Thread:** Clear monofilament.
**Tail:** A rabbit Zonker strip with strands of Krystal Flash.

**Body:** E-Z Body tubing.

**Eyes:** Small adhesive or dome eyes.

## Angel Deer'est/Atlantic Herring

**Hook:** Regular saltwater hook, size 2.

**Thread:** White 6/0 (140 denier).

**Body:** White bucktail, pearl Angel Hair, pearl Flashabou, blue Angel Hair, black Angel Hair, violet bucktail, and blue bucktail.

**Gills:** Red Angel Hair.

**Eyes:** Large silver dome eyes.

## Angel Deer'est/Green With Envy

**Hook:** Regular saltwater hook, size 2.

**Thread:** White 6/0 (140 denier).

**Body:** White bucktail, pearl Angel Hair, dark green Angel Hair, black Angel Hair, and chartreuse bucktail.

**Gills:** Red Angel Hair.

**Eyes:** Large silver dome eyes.

## Stealth Wing Streamer

**Hook:** Two regular saltwater hooks, size 2. Tie the hooks together and coat the thread wraps with superglue.

**Thread:** Clear monofilament.

**Tail:** Saddle hackle and strands of Flashabou, your choice of colors.

**Body:** Marabou, color to match the tail

**Eyes:** Medium dumbbell eyes.

## Ultra Bright Rattle Squid (Purple)

**Hook:** 6X-long saltwater hook, size 2.

**Thread:** Clear monofilament.

**Tail:** Long white and light dun saddle hackles with small bunches of pink and purple Angel Hair and tan Poly Bear or a similar kinky synthetic hair.

**Eyes:** Extra-large silver dome eyes glued to two strands of 60-pound-test monofilament.

**Body:** Large pearl E-Z Body on the back half of the hook shank, and a white bunny strip wrapped up the front half of the shank. Tie long bunches of tan Poly Bear and purple Angel Hair behind the hook eye.

**Note:** Tie a large rattle to the top of the hook shank before making the fly. The E-Z Body tubing covers the rattle. This is the purple version of the Ultra Bright Rattle Squid, but Capt. Stackelek also ties a pink version.

*Rabbit Eel*

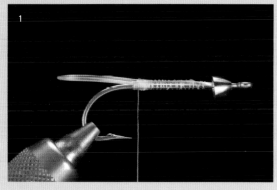

Slip a medium or large cone bead onto the hook. Start the thread, and tie a loop of 35-pound-test monofilament to the end of the hook shank. This mono will help prevent the tail of the fly from fouling around the hook.

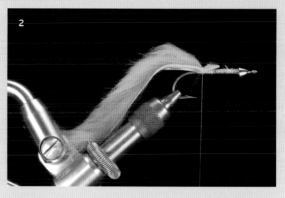

Tie a 3- to 5-inch-long rabbit strip to the hook.

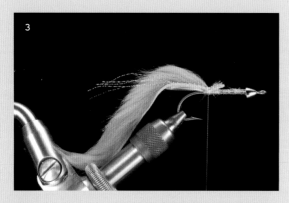

Tie a few strands of Krystal Flash to each side of the tail.

Add a tuft of rabbit fur to each side of the tail.

Tie a piece of large chenille to the hook. Wrap the chenille up the shank; don't crowd the metal bead. Tie off and clip the excess chenille.

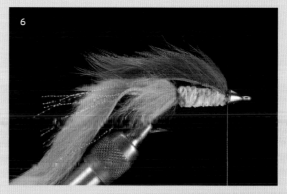

Tie on a rabbit strip to form the back of the fly. Tie off and clip the thread. Carefully coat the thread with a drop of cement.

Slip a piece of E-Z Body tubing onto the hook. Restart the thread behind the bead. Tie down the front end of the tubing. Tie off and clip the thread. Coat the tubing with five-minute epoxy. Allow the epoxy to harden before proceeding.

Tie a tuft of rabbit fur onto each side of the fly.

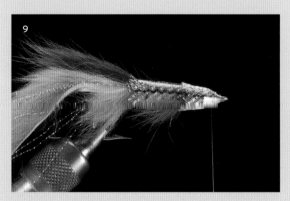

Slip a short piece of tubing on the hook to form the head of the fly. Okay, start the thread again; this time, right behind the hook eye. Tie down the front end of the tubing.

Tie off and clip the thread. Place an adhesive eye on each side of the head. Coat the head of the fly with epoxy.

# New York's David Nelson: Tying Without Rules

If you haven't heard of David Nelson, you will. David is a restaurant manager who lives in New York, and he is turning the fly-tying world on its head. David ties magnificent patterns that blend Flat-wings with the Spey school of fly tying. Just check out his flies on the following pages: I think they rank as some of the most beautiful that have ever been created.

David Nelson is only one of two tyers appearing in this book who is not a working guide. I am including him, however, because his patterns are so unique, and they are developing a reputation for catching large striped bass. Let me tell you about the first time I saw his flies.

I take many of the photographs of the flies that appear in *Saltwater Fly Fishing* magazine. One day, the editor of that great magazine, Steve Walburn, called to tell me about of a batch of flies he was sending for lens work.

"I'm shipping up a bunch of Flat-wings," he said. "I need some photos of them for the next issue of the magazine."

I was hesitant. Although Flat-wings certainly

catch fish, they often don't look good in print. They're so long and slender that you often have to place the camera far back to get the entire fly in the frame. As result, you sometimes get a photo of something that looks like a long pencil with a fish hook in the front.

"Do you really need to include a photo of Flat-wings?" I asked. "I just want to help you build a great looking article."

"Have you ever heard of David Nelson?"

"No," I replied.

"You haven't seen any of his flies?"

"No."

"Well, you need to check these out. They're pretty amazing."

The package arrived a few days later, and Steve was absolutely right; Nelson's flies were amazing. In fact, they almost took my breath away: I had never seen flies like these before; they were so long and colorful, and used feathers I had never seen on saltwater patterns. If I hadn't know better, I would have thought I was looking at some sort of mutant Atlantic salmon flies.

I'll bet David Nelson's flies will be new to you, too; he's just beginning to get the notoriety he so richly deserves. He is taking a whole new approach to tying striped bass flies; in this era of synthetic fly-tying materials, David is giving Flat-wings an Old World charm and beauty. And, after learning about what David calls Squimpish flies, I'll bet you will want to try your hand at tying some of these unusual patterns.

Even though he isn't a guide, I am happy to include David Nelson's patterns in this book. His work is very unusual, and I know you will enjoy my interview with him.

"I live in White Plains, New York, and predominantly fish in two places," David said at the beginning of our interview. "I fish Long Island Sound a lot, and for trout I go to the Upper Delaware River. For saltwater, I fish from Port Chester, New York, up to Southport, Connecticut. There are a lot of estuaries to fish; I tend to gravitate to the places that have a lot of current. At times I fish in a very urban setting. It's very interesting to catch stripers behind restaurants where people are having dinner

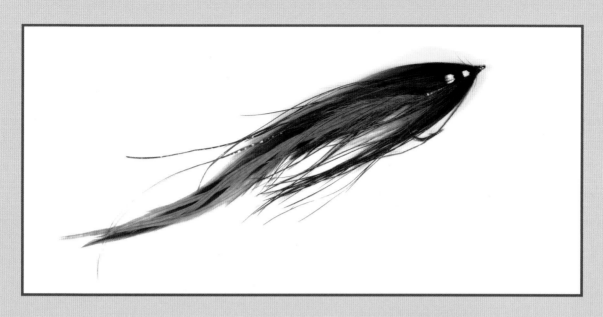

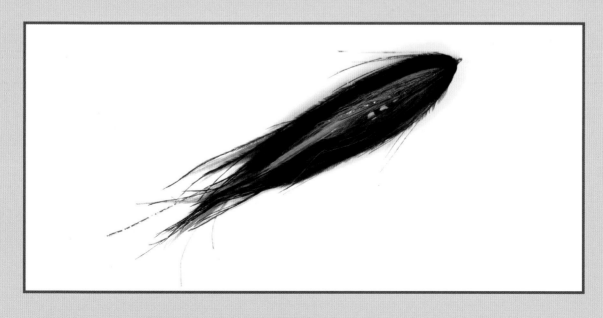

on a dock, and you're catching fish a hundred feet from them.

"I do a lot of wade fishing. If I'm lucky enough to hook up with someone who has a boat I'll get out on the water. For seven years I worked in Rowayton, Connecticut, which is right on the Five Mile River. The river dumps into Long Island Sound. It's an amazing place to meet people and fish for stripers. I fished off boats about three days a week."

You're really turning heads with your flies. How did you get started tying?

"I started tying trout flies. I went crazy with it. I read Vince Marinaro's *A Modern Dry Fly Code*. Then, I got an invitation to go out and fish for false albacore. I asked the guy what I needed to tie, and he showed me some stuff. I thought I'd try my hand at it, and I caught fish on my own flies. They were the ugliest creations."

Like a lot of us, Nelson started tying his own flies, thinking that it was a good way to save money.

"I just like to tie, and saltwater flies have always been expensive to buy, so I started making my own as a way to save money. Of course, fly tying really hasn't been less expensive, not by a long shot; it's easy to go overboard. But, a Deceiver at the store cost six bucks, and knew I could tie those; it's just bucktail and saddle hackles on a hook—no big deal. It just became something I love to do. I rarely fish other peoples' flies; I just like my flies more. I have more confidence in them."

Whether it's with his tying—which we'll fully explore in a moment—or fishing, David always marches to his own drummer.

"When someone tells me I shouldn't fish a certain way, that makes me want to do it all the more. Like, when I was told Montauk isn't a Flat-wing fishery, it made me want to do it all the more. The next day I caught triple the number of fish of anyone who was on our boat. I was using my flies. It got to the point other guys were demanding to try my flies, and they started catching more fish."

Coastal Connecticut is pretty heavily developed. How's the access for fishing?

"There's a fair amount of public access, especially if you're willing to walk a little bit, whether it is up or down a beach, or a quarter of a mile from the parking area to where the fishing is good. If you're fishing and not bothering people, a lot of times the security guard will look the other way. You get to know the local police; a lot of times they're interested in how the fishing is going, too."

How did you get the idea to tie these beautiful Flat-wing patterns?

"The first influence was Kenny Abrames. I read his book *Striper Moon*. I needed some new flies to solve the problem of fishing in currents where the bass were feeding but not remaining entirely stationary. The flies I had just weren't working very well. I was trying to dead-drift flies that were supposed to be stripped through the water—Deceivers and patterns tied with stiffer materials like Kinky Fiber. Then a friend showed me some Flat-wings, and I saw more on a Web site called stripermoon.com, and I started really thinking about the Flat-wing style of tying. I thought these might be the answer to my problem."

A lot of tyers try to replicate what they read in pattern recipes, but not David Nelson. Even when he was just starting out he used a recipe as a departure point, and then let his creative side take over.

"I didn't go crazy trying to exactly copy someone else's flies. I didn't count pieces of bucktail or hackles. I was more interested in the basic physics of the flies and how they'd behave in the water. I tied a few flies, and went to a reservoir by my house. I fish there a lot from a jon boat. I caught some great smallmouth bass that day; they struck when the flies were suspended between strips of line. It was unbelievable. They didn't want the Deceivers or Bunny patterns, they wanted a stationary Flat-wing."

You use a lot of materials I normally don't see on saltwater patterns.

"Yes, I love playing around with different and unusual materials. I use a lot of rhea on my flies. It's like ostrich herl, but it has less fluff on the individual fibers. I saw an article written by a Northwest steelhead guide named Paul Miller. He wrote about rhea, and included patterns for catching everything from trout to saltwater species. He included a couple of striper flies, and I thought this was a great material. I experimented with it for a year or so before I was happy, but it almost looks like Spey hackle."

That's exactly what I thought when I first saw your flies: Montauk meets the Spey River. The long rhea fibers give these flies a Spey flavor. It's like you put a kilt on Flat-wings.

"Even the really long fibers are burned rhea. I find some of that stuff on the Web. Try pillaging E-Bay, and look for sites for people who make hats. You can find all kinds of wild feathers that are excellent for fly tying. And some of the feathers I use are really very old. A lot of the people selling this stuff don't even know what it is. Last year a guy posted a photo of a batch of feathers; he didn't know what they were, but I recognized a lot of them. I couldn't believe what I got for forty bucks!"

You sent flies, but I didn't see any written recipes. Do you have actual patterns in mind when you tie, or do you experiment?

"No, I start with the basic Flat-wing style, and expand from there. The flies I've been tying lately have been really general imitations of big baitfish, but all the different feathers give them a lot of action."

Some of your flies are twelve and thirteen inches long. Do you actually use these for fishing?

"Absolutely."

But your intent isn't to imitate a specific baitfish. I mean, the colors of these flies are a little wild.

"If the fish are keying on big bait, I'll use one of those large flies. Let's say they're pushing around big bunker; every once in a while you'll see a large bass roll on the surface, and you know it's just come up on a bunker. One of those long flies is perfect for matching that baitfish. Other times they'll be going nuts on peanut bunker, but nothing seems to match the bait. If you drift your big fly through there, they'll suck it right in."

You keep talking about drifting these flies. Do you ever strip them through the water?

"Sometimes I do. Let's say you're quartering down with the current, I might give it a mend or two to get it to sink. I'll probably be fishing with a couple of split shot or a sinking head. As it tightens up with the swing, I'll give it a twitch or two to bring it to life, and then feed out some line. Sometimes the fish will strike when the fly is tight on the swing; other times they'll hit on the dead-drift, and you'll barely feel it."

So, you select a fly that matches the general size of the bait, right?

"Yes, that's the first step. If I can see some bait, or I know what's around, I'll try to 'match the hatch.'"

Does the color of the fly matter?

"I don't even pretend to know what the fish see. I don't think we, as humans, can even understand what the fish are really seeing. But I do like natural, drab colors. And I fish all-white flies; other times I fish all-black flies. For a couple of years I fished all-black patterns at night, and I caught fish. But then I switched to using flies that had some olive and purple in them, and I actually caught more fish. Sometimes I'll even fish with two flies at the same time—a light-colored fly and a dark fly—to see what the fish prefer. Sometimes the bass will definitely show a preference for a certain color, but I don't know why. Sometimes there's moonlight, other times there's not. Sometimes there is light from street lamps. Sometimes there's a shadow line on the water, and the fish will feed in the shadow, but not in the brighter area. It's all a big puzzle."

What type of tackle do you use to fish these flies?

"When I started I used the typical nine-weight rod. I switched to a six weight just for fun, but then I started catching some big fish and I was totally outgunned; it was stupid. About three years ago, I got into two-handed rods, and now I love them. I'm totally obsessed with them. They're great for fishing the beach, and a Spey rod is perfect for fishing in areas where you don't have a lot of room for a backcast."

Using a longer rod must really help to control the line when you want to fish the fly with a dead-drift.

"Oh yes, it really helps me to mend line. I usually use a twelve-foot long rod, and I occasionally step up to a fourteen footer, but the twelve-foot rod is my favorite. I'll use that really long rod when

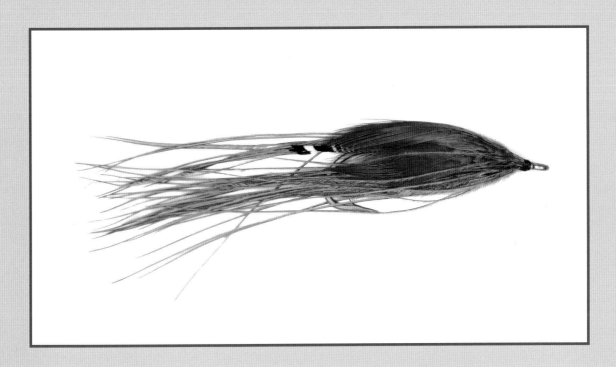

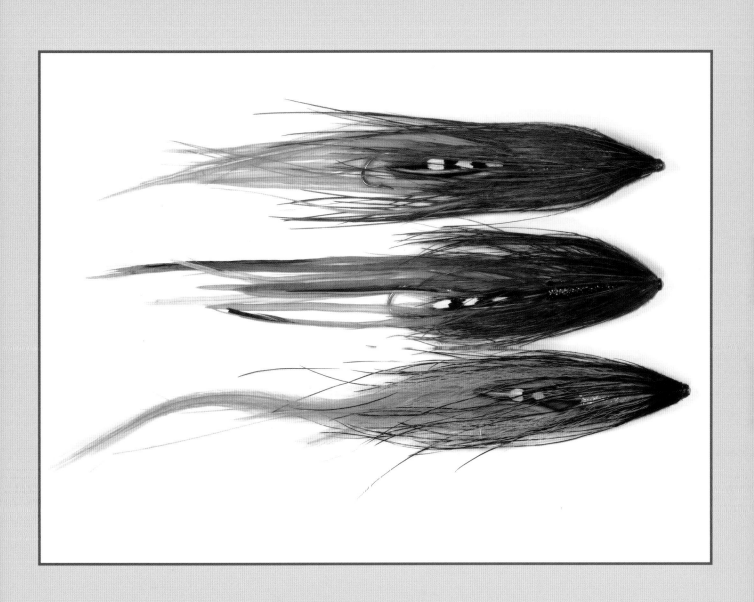

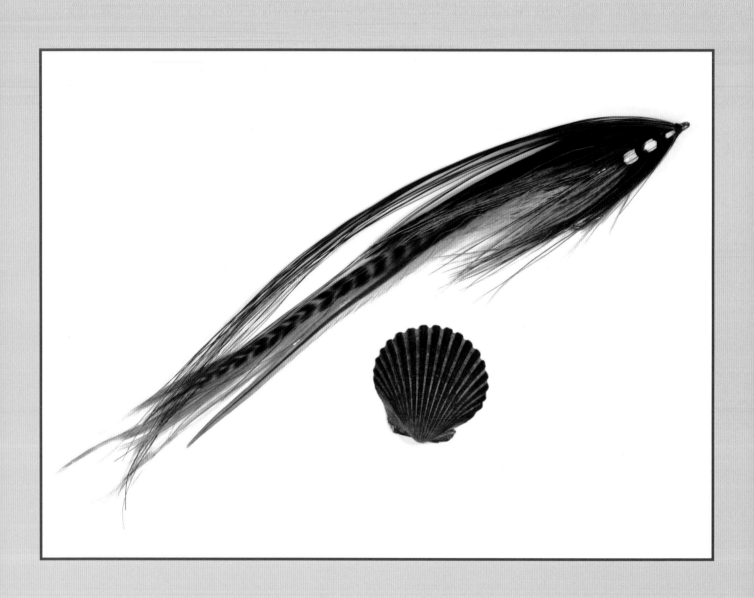

I'm looking for crazy distance. I can think of this one spot—I'm not giving anything up—I go to a golf course where the water floods in. It's got water areas that are at least eight feet deep at all times. When the tide comes in through this sluiceway, the fish line up in the main current seam. These are stripers. You're fishing in the middle of a golf course next to a river. You go there when the peanut bunker are around, in the middle of the day in mid-November, and the fish are blowing up on this bait! You wouldn't believe it: I'm casting from the putting green on the fourteenth hole. But sometimes the fish are one hundred feet out, and then I'll bring out that fourteen-foot rod. It's hilarious. But I did something stupid and went there on a Sunday and got in everybody's way, so now I go up on Tuesdays."

Let's use those peanut bunker as an example. Do you ever tie flies to match specific bait?

"I like to think that I tie some flies that imitate peanut bunker. Sometimes they have a wide belly, and I have a couple of flies that have Spey-style flat roofs and some hackle coming out under the belly. And I tie a lot of flies with Angel Hair over bucktail with saddle hackles. Those are definitely good baitfish imitations, whether it's mullet or whatever."

How long are those patterns?

"Seven to eight inches. I don't have any problem fishing a fly that is bigger than the bait. If the peanut bunker are four inches, I don't think there's anything wrong with fishing a six-inch fly."

Let's talk more about tackle. What kind of lines do you use?

"I use a lot of floating lines. I might add three or four feet of Rio T-14 to the end if I'm fishing a really heavy outflow. The Norwalk Islands has up to a ten-foot tide, so there can be some very strong currents. I change the line set-up to match the conditions. I might also add a couple pieces of split shot to get the fly down; other times I'll even have to add that sinking tip. And other times I've fished in rips off boats where I've used straight T-14; I'll put thirty feet of T-14 on an intermediate running line."

Fishing a fast current can be tough.

"I think a lot of people think they're fishing deeper than they really are. If you're fishing a two- or three-knot current, it's tough to get down unless you're stationary and casting upstream and mending line. But I've caught fish out of schools of bunker in fifteen to twenty feet of water."

You say you're fishing these flies with a dead-drift and then giving them just a slight amount of action. Do you cast up or across stream, and then mend? Exactly how do you do it?

"It depends on the area I'm fishing and the current. Let's say the bass are showing across and maybe slightly down-current from me. I'll cast across and then throw a couple of mends up with the current. This will allow the fly to settle down in the water. Then, I'll tighten the line when the fly gets maybe five feet from the fish. Here is where I want the fly to swing in front of them, and I'll give it a slight pumping action. When the fly pauses, it'll flare out and have more action. It's not just a straight swing through the water, but I do get a lot of strikes on the straight swing."

Let's talk more about the specifics of the flies. Some of these are really long: up to thirteen inches. What hook sizes do you use?

"From sizes 2/0 to 4/0."

What kind of hackles?

"I use a lot of Whiting hackles, and Keough hackles for some of the lighter colored feathers. These are really long saddle feathers. I was thrilled recently when Whiting Farms called and asked me to be on their pro staff. That was really nice of them. Whiting recently came out with their Flat-wing saddles, and they're great for what I do. And you need to check out the Internet. I find all kinds of amazing things from people who are selling feathers, but not necessarily for tying flies. You can get feathers with great quality, and not pay very much."

You don't have any defined patterns for your Flat-wings, but guys will still want to tie some of these flies and try them. Let's review the basic ingredients.

"I use long saddle hackles, bucktail, rhea, ostrich herl, peacock herl, Angel Hair, Flashabou, and some kind of braided body material if I think the body on the hook shank will show. You can even use jungle cock if you want. I tell people to use Kenny's method of tying a Flat-wing, but use your choice of materials. If you want to include yak or llama in the wing, then use these materials. If you want to palmer wrap a bunny strip at the front of the fly, then go for it. This is how it started for me: I thought Flat-wings were too wispy and thin at the front—they didn't have any bulk—so I started leaving room behind the hook eye and adding llama and Finnish raccoon at the front. Then I palmered a red hackle at the front, and I loved it."

And you like to layer materials on the hook.

"You bet. Nothing looks as good as a collar of bucktail, and over that you put Angel Hair, and over that you tie raccoon or llama or Icelandic sheep fleece. Brush these hairs back over the Angel Hair to get an amazing effect. Just get creative with what you already have on your tying bench. Anybody who can make a Woolly Bugger can tie my flies."

# TIER'S TUTORIAL: *Tying a Squimpish Fly*

This may be one of the most fun flies you'll tie in the entire book. It's completely free-style tying. There are no rules. Try to use the materials you already have on your tying bench and let your imagination run wild.

When I started to photograph the following tying sequence, I didn't know what colors or types of materials I would use. But I knew I wanted to use only common materials; the sort of things you'll find in any fly shop. First, I had to tie the tail of the fly. I dipped into my stash of Whiting Farms schlappen and found some bold yellow feathers. I decided to use six of these, three feathers per side. I also selected two coq de Leon feathers; I would flank each side of the tail with one of these feathers. Finally, I plucked two body feathers from a ring-necked pheasant skin; these would look great tied to the base of the tail.

The body is yellow and fiery brown Partridge SLF Hanks. I blended together a small bunch of each color, and inserted them in a dubbing loop. I then wrapped the long dubbing fibers up the hook, and tied off and clipped the excess loop. Next, I picked and brushed back the fibers.

David Nelson uses rhea on many of his flies, but this is not a material you'll find in many fly shops. Black bucktail is an admirable substitute for rhea, or you might want to use marabou or ostrich herl.

David Nelson's flies are unusual, but they are also very beautiful. They follow no rules, and guess what: The fish don't mind a bit.

Start the thread on the hook. Stack and tie on the hackles to form the tail of the fly. Use your choice and length of hackles.

Tie on strands of holographic Flashabou or your choice of flash material.

(tying steps continue on the next page)

I tied a pheasant "church window" body feather on each side of the tail.

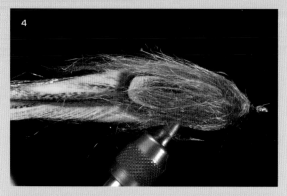

A blend of spun dubbing wrapped on the hook creates an interesting effect.

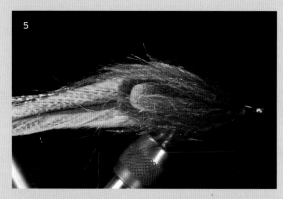

Tying on small bunches of bucktail adds bulk to the front of the fly.

Tie off and clip the thread.

# Capt. Jim Ellis Puts
# the Meaning in "Home Waters"

8

*I* first encountered Capt. Jim Ellis when writing a book titled *Guide Flies*, which was also published by Countryman Press. That particular book contains a blend of both freshwater and saltwater patterns. I was particularly attracted to Capt. Ellis' striped bass and bluefish flies. They were beautifully tied and very practical. Several of them are tied on circle hooks; circle hooks were fairly new at that time, at least to fly tyers, and I wanted to learn more about them. I called Jim and conducted a quick interview. During that discussion, he mentioned the fact that he had an ancestor that was on the *Mayflower*. His family's history, as well as his flies, stuck in my mind, so when it came time to do the research for this book, it was only natural to include him.

I caught up with Capt. Ellis in the middle of November. His fishing season was winding down, and he was packing the truck to go deer hunting in Maine. I was glad he had time to talk.

"I just finished all my chores. The truck is packed and I'm ready to go. We have a camp in Maine. If I'm not thinking about hunting, I'm thinking about fishing."

I remember that the last time we spoke you mentioned the fact that your family has lived on Cape Cod for several generations.

"I'm the thirteenth generation living on Cape Cod. There was an Ellis on the *Mayflower*. My father has researched it; he's an historian and has written several books on Cape Cod and New England history. Our people have lived here a very long time."

So, you obviously guide around Cape Cod. With your family's history, you sort of give a new meaning to the term "home waters."

"I mostly fish Cape Cod Bay, and some in Vineyard Sound, depending upon wind conditions and the time of the season. But I spend three-quarters of my time in Cape Cod Bay; the rest of it is on Vineyard Sound and the south side of the Cape. When I'm fishing the bay, I go out of Barnstable Harbor. It's almost dead center in the bottom of the bay, so wherever the fish are, from Cape Cod Canal up toward Wellfleet and to Brewster, I'm right in the middle and can get to them."

When do you start guiding?

"We generally start fishing from between the fif-teenth to the twentieth of May. You can fish earlier than that, but it's not consistent enough; usually the weather isn't as cooperative, and some years the fish are here and other years they're not. For consistency, the second to third week of May is a good time to start taking clients fishing."

What type of bait do you have early in the season?

"Early on we have quite a few herring and alewives, and the mackerel show up. The bass are also chasing sand eels. The last couple of years, we've been having a much better run of squid in the bay than we've had in the past. It's pretty cool. You'll see gannets on the flats; that's usually an ocean bird, but they come in to chase the squid. And as you know, the bass can act really stupid when the squid are around.

"The squid will go wherever the sand eels go. They'll get up in some very shallow water. Some of those flats are exposed sand at low tide, but at high tide there is eight to nine feet of water. It's the lower portion of the Gulf of Maine, and we get a nine-and-a-half-foot tide. On the south side of the Cape you get only a three- to three-and-a-half-foot tide. It's two different worlds. Around the moon phases we can get twelve-foot tides—a big exchange of water."

With such large tides, you must really have to gauge your fishing around the tides.

"Absolutely, but you can find fish on any tide. But, when the tide goes out, it's like somebody pulled a plug in a bathtub and there aren't as many places to be on the flats. On the other hand, this can restrict the fish to certain areas, and the fishing can actually be better. The other part of it is that the current can really speed up, and line control is very important; you cast a fly, and before you know it, it's whipped right back before you can get even a couple of strips."

So what do you do?

"For the most part, I'll have two clients on board, and one guy might not be getting a good shot at the fish. A lot of times I'll edge the boat up to a corner or eddy and tie off the anchor line from the center console. This way we can go side-to and both guys can get some good fishing."

How big are the first stripers of the season?

"We start with some big fish right off the bat. I think some real little fish come in mid- to late April, but by the time I start guiding until the Fourth of July, we'll see real nice fish in the areas that are conducive to fly fishing. But you can never tell: Different migrations of bass come and go, but we usually get some very nice fish early on."

What's the most common mid-summer bait?

"Mid-summer we have sand eels, shrimp, and crabs. By that time I'm doing a lot more wading and sight fishing. It's difficult to do conventional sight fishing on those flats just because the current is moving so fast. If you see a fish, all you can do is turn the boat one way or the other so you have a better cast with the wind; you can't pole against the strong current. For the most part, you wait until the tide drops to where you can wade. I get the client out of the boat, point out the slot, and tell them what I expect the fish to do. I let them wade it on their own. I stay with the boat because the current is moving so much and you don't want the boat to float away or get high and dry. Sometimes, I'll go with them if I think I can, but again, it depends upon the conditions. We'll fish an area for half an hour and then move up tide or down tide depending upon the direction of the flow. We'll fish three or four different flats, and by that time the tide is either gone or totally full. The clients wear their stripping baskets and waders, and it works out very well. You can't even do this on your own because you have to stick with your boat."

When does your season wind down?

"I usually fish until about October twentieth or Halloween, depending upon the fall storms. There's still some fish around through November, but there are no great numbers. They're chasing silversides on the bay side, and of course the peanut bunker. In some years you can go out a little farther and get into schooling bluefin tuna. You might get a run of bay anchovies, and we also get some adult bunker; these run two to two-and-a-half feet in length. They attract some really big bass."

Do you switch to fishing the south side of Cape Cod in the autumn?

"I play that by the wind. It depends upon which way the wind is blowing. When it's coming out of the north, I'll fish the south side, and vice versa. There are plenty of fish in both spots, so you rarely get blown out. There's always some place to go; especially

on the south side, there are a lot of little bays and places where you can tuck in out of the wind."

What type of fly do you use to fish the flats?

Guzzle Bug

"The Guzzle Bug is an all-around crab or shrimp imitation. I use that for sight fishing on the flats. I wanted something that I could tie very quickly and would have a lot of movement in the water. That's cross-cut rabbit for the body and craft fur for the tail. For the most part, when those fish come up on the flats, the predominant bait is sand eels, but for whatever reason, they don't key on sand eels, they're looking for shrimp and crabs. The Guzzle Bug works far better than a sand eel pattern on the flats. You can do all right with a sand eel pattern, but it needs to be tied very sparse. And when you're wading, your fly should have very little or no flash; a flashy fly spooks the fish."

What kind of line do you use to fish the flats?

"A floater or a clear intermediate-sinking line. You can use a floating line and get away with it most of the time; I use one because it's quick to pick up off the water to make the next cast. But sometimes the fish get real picky and a clear intermediate line is the way to go. The length of leader depends upon the mood of the fish; if they're spooky, use a longer leader.

"I always use a fluorocarbon tippet because it's less visible in the water. Sometimes, if it's a beautiful day with a light north wind, those fish will not eat. You can have the most perfect presentation, the fly will drop to the water way ahead of a fish, and the bass will swim right up to the fly; but, once it sees the slightest movement from the pattern, it will take off. This is when you have to use everything you can to reduce the visibility of your tackle, or you'll keep spooking fish."

You sent two versions of the Tuna Melt.

*Tuna Melt*

"Yes, and it's also tied with cross-cut rabbit and Angel Hair. I first tied it to catch bluefin tuna when they're feeding on peanut bunker or small herring. The hardest thing is to tie a fly that is small enough and still has enough action on a hook that it large enough to handle one of those fish. I tie that on size 3/0 and 4/0 hooks. But the Tuna Melt also works for

catching striped bass."

What about the Mosquetucket Eel: where does the name come from?

"Mosquetucket is where I fish in Barnstable. 'Mosque' is the Native-American name for Sandy Neck Beach, and 'tucket' means 'end of land.' Those flats are full of sand eels. The tail is white bucktail, and I tie in the tan bucktail pointing forward over the hook eye. I then tie on Bill's Bodi Braid, and wrap the body; the completed body is three layers of Bodi Braid. I like to coat the body with thinned Dave's Flexament; I want the thinned glue to penetrate all the way to the hook. Next, I fold the tan hair back like a Thunder Creek, and cinch it down with clear monofilament thread. I also make a few wraps of clear thread over the adhesive eyes so they conform to the curve of the head. The thread disappears when you coat the body with epoxy."

You tie a lot of flies on circle hooks.

"A lot of people who are somewhat new to the sport sometimes have difficulty setting the hook, especially when using a small, light pattern like the Mosquetucket Eel. You know how a bass is: It'll suck the fly right back into its gills, and then turn and take off. Some new anglers don't even know the fish has taken the fly until it turns, and then it's hooked in the gills and will die. Circle hooks really do reduce hooking mortality, and the inexperienced anglers still catch fish. I tie the Mosquetucket Eel on a size two circle hook."

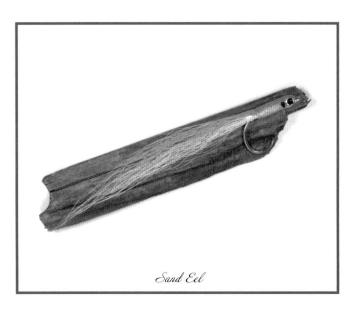

*Sand Eel*

*Ellis Anchovy*

The Ellis Anchovy is a neat little pattern.

"I tie that fly using several layers of Bill's Bodi Braid. Since I wrap so many layers, I have to take extra precaution to keep the material from slipping around. I'll wrap a layer and squeeze it, then tighten it with my thumb and forefinger. I'll also make a few wraps of clear monofilament thread to lock it in place. I'll keep adding layers of Bodi Braid in this way to build up the body of the fly. I also coat the body with very thin Dave's Flexament; it's about twenty-five percent glue and seventy-five percent thinner. I want the cement to penetrate the Bodi Braid right down to the hook shank. I tie the Ellis Anchovy on a slightly larger hook to accommodate the thickness of the body; I don't want the belly to reduce the hook gap. I originally tied the Ellis Anchovy in a darker color for the schooling bluefin tuna. I also use it for schooling albies when they are chasing bay an-

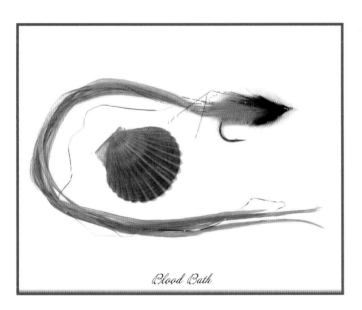

Blood Bath

chovies; I just tie it in lighter colors."

The Blood Bath is the final fly you sent. It's almost a foot long. What do you use this for?

"In the spring, everybody keys in on the worm hatch. Well, little worms come from big worms. Fishermen look at the moon phases to figure out when there will be a worm hatch. A week or two before the hatch, the big worms come up on the high tide; they swim around, mate, and do their thing. Anywhere there's a mud bottom where you'd expect to have a worm hatch, you'll find big bass daisy chained,

feeding on those big worms."

But this fly is almost a foot long. Are the real worms this long?

"Sea worms are like accordions, and they pulse along when they swim. You'll see them in the water, and they can be incredibly long. We were trying to figure out what those big bass were doing, and then I saw some sea worms swim by. It was obvious: The stripers were keying in on the big worms. When I was little, my grandfather trolled big sea worms with spinners and little beads. That's all they used in May, and the old timers caught tons of big bass. You still might find a worm-trolling rig in a tackle shop around here. But the Blood Bath is a specific fly for using maybe four or five days out of the year. The worm hatch is usually on the new moon, so you're using this pattern a week or so before that. Look for the big bass. You'll see them. They look like laid-up tarpon a foot or so below the surface."

How do you fish those big flies? Do you use an active retrieve?

"Don't anchor the boat; just drift. Use a floating or clear intermediate-sinking line, and sight fish to the bass. Cast right to them and see what happens. They are really picky when they're feeding on the large worms, but these are big fish and worth the effort. Get the fly to pulse with long strips, and let it flutter in the water. These flies don't require a lot of action; the movement of the feathers gets their attention.

"The hardest part about using the Blood Bath is not getting the long hackles fouled around the hook. If you look real close, you'll see that the feathers are threaded through a narrow loop of monofilament. This helps keep them from fouling. I tie hackles to the hook, then tie on the loop. Next, narrow the loop with wraps of clear thread. Finally, pull the feathers through the back of the loop. I restrict the size of the loop to prevent the hackles from migrating forward when casting or fishing the fly."

**Blood Bath**
**Hook:** Regular length saltwater hook, size 2/0.
**Thread:** Black 6/0 (140 denier).
**Tail:** Extra-long tan dry-fly saddle hackles and two long strands of green Flashbou. Tie a loop of 30-pound-test monofilament at the end of the

hook shank to help prevent the hackles from fouling around the hook.

**Body:** A tan cross-cut rabbit strip wrapped up the hook shank, and four or five short strands of green Flashabou.

**Head:** Tufts of black rabbit fur.

### Mosquetucket Sand Eel

**Hook:** Regular or short-shank saltwater hook, size 2.

**Thread:** Clear monofilament.

**Tail:** Tan and white bucktail.

**Body:** Pearl braid.

**Eyes:** Small silver adhesive eyes.

**Gills:** Red permanent marker.

**Note:** Coat the body of the fly with epoxy.

### Tuna Melt

**Hook:** Regular or short-shank saltwater hook, size 2/0.

**Thread:** Clear monofilament.

**Tail:** Narrow pearl E-Z Body or olive Angel Hair.

**Body:** White rabbit fur.

**Eyes:** Large silver dome eyes.

### Guzzle Bug

**Hook:** Regular or short-shank saltwater hook, size 6 or 4.

**Thread:** Brown 6/0 (140 denier).

**Weight:** Medium lead dumbbell.

**Tail:** Tan Silli Legs or craft fur.

**Body:** A tan cross-cut rabbit strip wrapped around the hook shank.

### Ellis Anchovy

**Hook:** Short-shank saltwater hook, size 2.

**Thread:** Clear monofilament.

**Back and tail:** Gold Angel Hair.

**Body:** Pearl braid.

**Eyes:** Medium white adhesive eyes.

**Gills:** Red permanent marker.

**Note:** Coat the body with epoxy.

# TIER'S TUTORIAL: *Tying the Guzzle Bug*

Start the thread on the hook. Tie on a medium dumbbell.

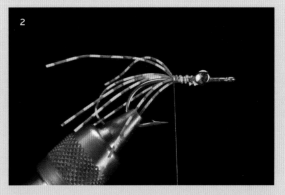

Tie on several rubber legs or a pinch of craft fur.

Tie on a rabbit strip. Wrap the strip up the hook shank. Pass the strip over the dumbbell on the top of the fly. (That's the side with the hook point.) Make one or two wraps in front of the dumbbell. Tie off and clip the excess rabbit strip.

Tie off and clip the thread. Coat the thread wraps with cement.

# Joseph O'Clair
# Goes into the Fly Business

his book contains the flies of two people who are not actual fishing guides. The first was New York's David Nelson; that's the young chap who ties the incredibly colorful—and big—Squimpish flies. I am including him because he's a young tier, and he also works outside the box; David follows no rules when he sits down to the vise, and I think that's cool.

Joseph O'Clair is the second non-guide tier I consulted when researching this book. I am including Joe because he ties nice flies, and perhaps more importantly, he represents the fly-fishing "everyman." He isn't trying to use fly-fishing as a means to earn a living: He doesn't whisk clients around in an expensive boat, he doesn't write about his adventures, nor does he do any of the other typical things the "pros" do. Joe is a retired chef turned professional fly tier,

and when you talk with him, you get the distinct impression that making a dollar is the last thing on his mind when he sits down to the vise. He reminds us that the objective of fly tying is to have fun.

What were you doing before you started your fly-tying business? I asked as we began getting acquainted.

"I was working up to eighty hours a week, and when I retired, I went down to zero hours per week. I was driving my wife nuts. After the first year she said, 'Hey, find something to do with yourself. You're driving me crazy walking around the house all day.' I mean, I was fishing, but you can fish only so much."

How did you get into fly tying?

"One day I saw an ad in the newspaper about a fly tying demo. I pointed it out to her, and she said, 'You used to tie flies. Why don't you go?' It sounded interesting. I went to the demo that night and sat in the front row, and took a lot of notes. After the seminar, I went up to talk with the guy who was tying. We had a nice conversation. He asked if I was a tier, and I said I'd tied flies when I was about sixteen years old. But, like I said, you get a little older and have to do things like work to put kids through college, and you kind of have to put the toys away; I didn't have the time, but I thought I'd like to get back into it. He was very nice and gave me a lot of good leads. So, I went home with a ton of notes, and decided to pursue it.

"The first thing I did was write to the materials companies and a lot of people I didn't even know. I had lots of questions about what they had in the way of materials and if they had any samples, and before you knew it the mailbox was full every day. These companies were really great about it."

What kind of flies did you tie when you were young?

"I tied freshwater flies when I was a kid, so I started researching saltwater flies. I started tying, and went to a few seminars. I took my flies to the seminars for the pros to look at and critique. I wanted them to tell me what I was doing right, and where I could make improvements. I got a lot of good information, both pro and con. You've got to go in with an open mind and just be ready to learn.

"I was tying flies and testing them, and, by God, we were catching fish with them. I gave some flies to

*Brown Squid*

*Real Eels*

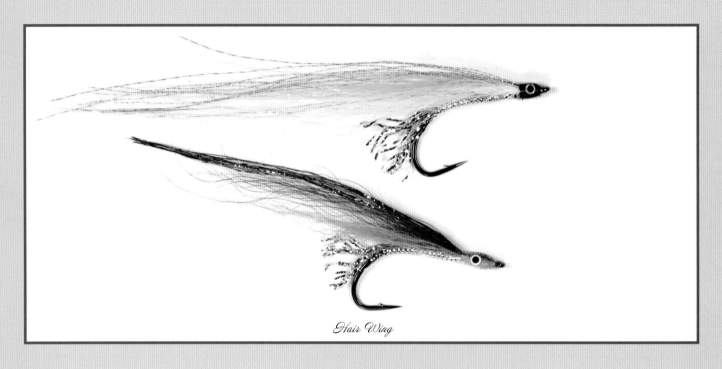

*Hair Wing*

*Large Squid*

my buddies, and they started catching fish with them. Other people started asking me where I was getting my flies. When I told them I tied them, they asked if I could tie some for them. I was telling these guys they could have whatever I had in the box, no problem. The first year I was just giving them away. The next year I started tying some different patterns, and it worked out better than the first year."

How did you decide to turn your hobby into a business?

"One day I was in my accountant's office, and when we were done with our business, she asked what I had been doing. I told her I'd been tying a lot of flies. Well, it just so happened that there was a woman in her office who fly-fished, and she over-heard this. She came into the office and we started talking about fishing. I told her I had some of my flies in the car, and I brought them in. She really liked them and offered to buy a couple dozen, but I told her just to take them. My accountant, however, said I should go into business. I asked her how to do that, and she said she'd handle all the legal paperwork and get all the credentials from the State of Massachusetts. She said, however, that she would need the name of the company, and without thinking twice, I said 'Fly-catcher.' She said that was a pretty good name, and that was the birth of Flycatcher Saltwater Flies. That was about seven years ago."

How was business? Was it hard to get people to buy your flies?

"The first year I went around to the shops with some samples, told them what I was doing, and asked if they'd like to buy any. I told them I was taking or-ders. Some of them placed some nice orders. The second year I expanded my repertoire with more patterns, and some of the shops reordered; they said that they had sold my flies before any of the others. That was real nice.

"Next, I took a computer class at the local adult-ed school. I quickly saw the potential of using it for the fly tying business. I decided to set up an album of my flies, so I bought a digital camera. I hooked it up to the computer and a printer, and I photographed all my flies. I set up a photo album of my flies on the computer. I added notes about the hook brands and sizes, the materials used to tie each fly, and so on. I then printed all this off, and had my album. Now, when I visit my customers, I can take this book that contains all my flies. It's about thirty pages long.

"First, when you go into a store, the guy is pretty dubious. In most stores, fly-fishing is just a secondary means of income to supplement the bait and the rods and reels. A lot of them carry flies and fly tackle, but it's just enough for the fly fisherman who might come in, but it's not their main business. So, I would tell them to just look through my album. Well, some of these guys would spend twenty or thirty minutes reading it, and they'd start placing orders: 'Give me two dozen of these, and give me three dozen of those, and give me some Clousers. And do them in these colors.' So, that's where I am now. Rather than walking around with a few flies in my pocket, I can show them everything I do, I can tell them what I already have in stock, and I tell them I can tie these flies in any special colors they might want. It's great, and I've met some really nice people. I sell flies to several shops on the Cape."

Do you ever tie flies for individuals?

"Oh sure, I get calls from locals who want me to tie flies for them. They'll ask for very specific things, like they want their flies to have longer tails, or they'll ask for a little extra flash, and things like that. That's no problem. I consider myself a custom fly tier; I'll do anything you want. My customers seem happy with my flies, and they're catching a lot of fish with them."

You obviously create a lot of your own patterns. Are you still experimenting with new ideas?

Squid

"Yes I am. Lately, I've been working on some bigger, seven- to eight-inch-long flies. Last year we had a lot of football tuna in the area, and a couple of guys who had ten-weight rods wanted to go after them. I tied a squid that I know was perfect for them. I wrapped the hook shank full of lead wire so that it would sink quickly and get past the bluefish.

"I tie smaller squid, too. Every situation calls for a different fly. I think the weather can determine what will work best—sun or clouds, wind or calm water. And then there are the ability and tastes of the angler; some guys can't cast larger flies, or they like using flies of a certain size or color."

You sent an orange and a white squid. Do you do this in different colors?

"No, I do that only in orange and white. That's funny how that fly came about. I met a friend of mine who fishes Monomoy Island, and I asked him what he used. He said a big, orange squid pattern. He showed it to me, and I told him I could tie something better than what he was using. So, I came home and tied two dozen for him. He later called and said they were working great; they were like giving candy to a kid. Every year he orders two or three dozen; he doesn't fish with anything else.

"Some people think an orange fly doesn't work, but up there it really works. I have a theory about that. I talked with a guy who wanted a fly with an orange body and a red wing. He caught some nice bass on it, and he claimed that it's because the fly imitates the colors of the lobsters in that area. He pointed out that the lobstermen have to throw the short lobsters back in the water, and he said those lobsters never reach the bottom; the bass get them. He said there's always a trail of bass following the lobster boat. But, no one else wants an orange fly, so I started tying it in white."

Do you have any tips for beginning tyers?

"When learning to tie, one of the first questions you have to answer is where are you going to use your flies. Are you fishing in an inlet, or offshore, or around rocks? For instance, if you're fishing in an estuary of a river, I'd recommend that you tie something like a small Clouser or a small sand eel. This is because the bait in an estuary is usually small. If you fish in the ocean, you'll want to use a larger fly be-cause the bass are looking for bigger bait. And I'd add more flash to an ocean fly so the fish can easily see it.

"I know the fly designers used to go over to the factories and show the production people how to tie the flies, but the person who's tying those flies has never even seen the fish the angler is trying to catch. That, to me, is a disappointment. If you're a fish-erman, you're going to tie a more realistic fly than the person who just says, 'Well, I saw this picture, and I'm just going to duplicate it.'"

Do you ever try to catch samples of the bait you're imitating?

"Oh sure. I have a big seine net. Sometimes, when my ten-year-old grandson comes up, we throw out the net and see what we can catch. I explain to him what we find. Very importantly, from my perspective, I spend a lot of time examining the various colors and shapes of the bait. Sometimes I take a photo-graph of the bait, and I put the picture on my tying table while I work. After about ten or fifteen tries, the fly comes out pretty close to matching the bait. I al-ways tell new tyers that not every fly will come out right. I still have a box of flies that I tied maybe fif-teen years ago, and you look at them and say 'my God, who tied these.' As you tie on a regular basis, you just get better.

"You should set up a place with a vise, and leave it set up all the time. And don't try to tie a fly all in one session; you can do it in stages. Like with Clousers: I tie and glue the dumbbell eyes on a whole batch of hooks. Then I'll tie tails on the hooks and glue those

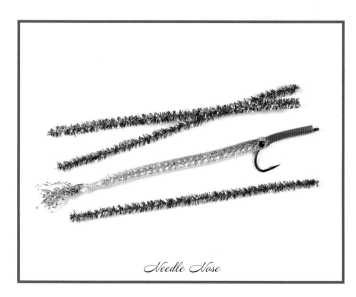

*Needle Nose*

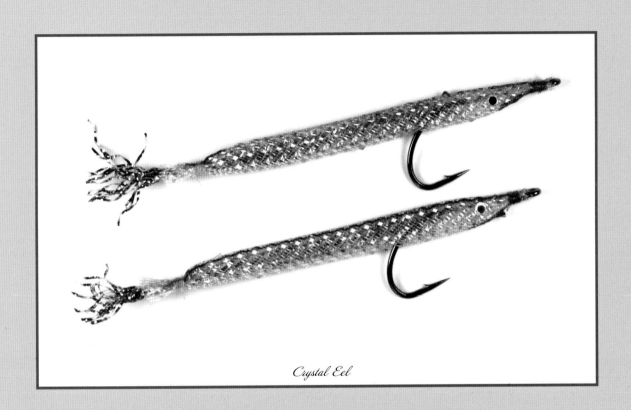

*Crystal Eel*

down. Finally I can go back and finish all the flies. And I'll apply three or four coats of cement to the heads so they can withstand a lot of punishment."

This Needle Nose is a really unusual pattern.

"There's a story behind the Needle Nose. I was talking to guy who said these funny-looking fish were trailing his plug all the time, and all of a sudden a bluefish would come up and nail them. I live on the Bass River, and I told him that he was seeing needle nose. He asked what a needle nose was, and I told him it looked a lot like a baby gar. He said that was it.

"It was sort of a joke, but I told the guy I'd make some flies for him that would imitate a needle nose, but that I'd make them bright and flashy. He asked what he was supposed to do with them, and I said he should use them as trailers behind the plug. After a couple of weeks he asked for some more. He said the bluefish were just sucking them down; they'd come up behind the plug and nail the fly. I don't know if it's the color or it's something that just annoys them, but they really hit it.

"Well, I started tying and selling the Needle Nose. I tie on a piece of 40-pound-test monofilament as a bite tippet, and package it in an envelope. You can use the Needle Nose as a trailer behind a plug or as an individual fly. The fly shops put them up by the cash registers, and when the guys are buying their plugs or bait, they say they'll take one or two Needle Noses. It's been a great sales item. Some things are just accidental."

*Joe's Bead Head*

Tell me about Joe's Bead Head.

"Joe's Bead Head was my idea. I was fishing off the dock, and the schoolies were just under the surface. My flies are either sitting on the water or going down deep, and I needed something that would fish just under the surface. I saw a similar fly in *Fly Tyer* magazine for fishing in fresh water, and I knew there was nothing like it for saltwater. So, I created Joe's Bead Head Fly. I made two or three, and they didn't look right, so I did them over and experimented with some different ideas. When you strip it through the water—just under the surface—it cuts a nice V wake. It's the first saltwater bead fly I've seen on the market, and I passed them out to some of the local guys, and they started catching fish with it."

What kind of beads do you use?

"Believe it or not, I went to the hobby shop and purchased nine-millimeter plastic beads. You get something like five hundred beads for two dollars; they cost next to nothing. I put them on pins and spray them with a little color to give them some highlights. It's a very simple fly to make, and it's very sparse. And it makes a nice wake that attracts fish; I think the fish look up, see the wake, and they hit it. I fish it with an eight-weight floating line."

Do you get a lot of time on the water to test your flies?

"I get around and fish a lot of water. I fish the Bass River, Monomoy, and down around Hyannis. I just like to get out, especially early in the morning. I put on my waders, walk out and start casting. I usually miss my first fish because I'm looking at the birds and enjoying the scenery; the first strike is the wakeup call. I also like to fish at night. If the tide and water is right, I'll use a floating line and popper—something that'll stay on the surface."

What other tips can you give new tyers?

"I tell guys to start with something like a Clouser. Just start with one fly, and learn how to tie it properly. And tie it all season. Really learn that fly, but don't be afraid to experiment with it. Tie it in a wide variety of colors, and add a lot of flash. And get out there and fish it and really work it.

"One of the problems with new fly tyers is that they jump around from fly to fly, and they never master any of them. Then they become discouraged.

I think a new tier should learn how to make a proven pattern, and then go out and catch fish with it. That's the best way to learn and get confidence.

"When it comes to actual tying, I tie all of my flies wet; I moisten everything with a sponge. For instance, when working with bucktail, I wet the hair and pick out the short and stray fibers. When the fly is finished it's actually wet. Why? Because this is the profile it will have when it's in the water being fished. And if you work with dry bucktail, you're going to build up a certain amount of static electricity and the hair is going to want to stand straight up on you. I tried all kinds of things to eliminate the static electricity, even the spray stuff the gals use to keep their skirts from sticking to their stockings. But if you moisten your fingers and then stroke the materials, or moisten the materials with a wet sponge, you can better control the materials and get a better idea how the fly will look in the water. This is one of the little techniques I teach in my tying class. And by the way, I never put the materials in my mouth to moisten them. I see some guys put the feathers in their mouths, but you don't know where they've been or what chemicals are on them."

### Realistic Sand Eel
**Hook:** Regular saltwater hook, size 1.
**Thread:** Clear monofilament.
**Underbody:** Silver braid wrapped on the hook shank.
**Tail:** Four pieces of gold thread tied on the hook shank before wrapping the body. The thread extends through the body tubing to form the tail of the fly.
**Body:** A 3-inch-long piece of natural Bill's Bodi Braid. Color the body with olive and black permanent markers.
**Eyes:** Small silver adhesive eyes coated with epoxy.

### Squid
**Hook:** Regular saltwater hook, size 1.
**Thread:** Size 6/0 (140 denier), color to match the body.
**Tail:** Six to eight orange saddle hackles with four or five strands of narrow gold Flashabou, or

six to eight white saddle hackles with four or five strands of narrow pearl Flashabou.
**Collar:** Gray marabou.
**Body:** Orange or white chenille.
**Head:** Orange or white wool combed back.
**Eyes:** Medium silver dome eyes glued to the sides of the body.

### Large Squid–Tuna Series
**Hook:** Gamakatsu 55015-25, size 5/0.
**Thread:** Clear monofilament.
**Tail:** Eight long white saddle hackles and pearl Flashabou.
**Collar:** Purple bucktail, red bucktail, and purple Flashabou.
**Body:** Pearl Bill's Bodi Braid.
**Eyes:** Large pink dome eyes.
**Nose:** Fold back the body material to form the front of the squid. Note the additional strands of purple and red Flashabou.

### Joe's Bead Head Fly
**Hook:** Regular saltwater hook, size 1.
**Thread:** Clear monofilament.
**Head:** 9-millimeter craft store bead.
**Tail:** Narrow silver Mylar tubing.
**Wing:** Bucktail.
**Throat:** Red calftail.
**Note:** Joe's Bead Head Fly is a very adaptable pattern. Select materials in your choice of colors.

### Crystal Sand Eel
**Hook:** Regular saltwater hook, size 1.
**Thread:** Clear monofilament.
**Body:** 3-inch-long piece of pearl Bill's Bodi Braid. Color the back of the body with an olive permanent marker, and color the mouth with a red marker.
**Tail:** 2-inch-long piece of gold tinsel purchased at a hobby shop; the material resembles a pipe cleaner. Insert the material into the end of the body, and secure the end of the tubing with tight wraps of thread.
**Eyes:** Extra-small silver adhesive eyes coated with epoxy.

## Needle Nose

**Hook:** Regular saltwater hook, size 1.

**Thread:** Clear monofilament.

**Underbody:** Gold or silver tinsel stem with a wire core. Spray the top of the stem in your choice of color; the bottom of the stem, which forms the belly of the fly, should remain silver or gold.

**Body:** Small or medium E-Z Body tubing.

**Tail:** Silver or gold braid.

**Eyes:** Small silver or gold dome eyes.

**Nose:** A 1-inch-long piece of 3/16-inch-diameter plastic tubing. Select a color to match the color of the underbody.

## Brown Squid

**Hook:** Long shank saltwater hook, size 1.

**Thread:** Clear monofilament.

**Tail:** Eight brown or brown grizzly hackles, four tied on each side of the hook, and strands of lavender Flashabou.

**Body:** White Flashabou, coated with a thin layer of head cement.

**Eyes:** Medium silver dome eyes.

**Flash:** Three strands of lavender Flashabou, folded over the thread and tied behind the hook eye.

## Hair Wing

**Hook:** Regular saltwater hook, size 1.

**Thread:** Clear monofilament or black 6/0 (140 denier).

**Tail and body:** Silver braid. Force the braid over the hook eye. Unravel the end of the braid to form the tail of the fly. Tie off the braid at both ends of the hook shank.

**Wing:** Bucktail and strands of Flashabou and Krystal Flash.

**Eyes:** Extra-small silver adhesive eyes.

# TIER'S TUTORIAL: *Tying the Realistic Sand Eel*

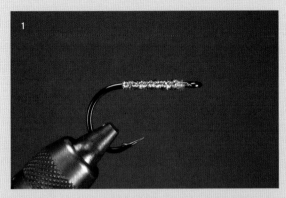

Start the thread on the hook. Tie a piece of flashy braid to the end of the hook shank. Wrap the thread to the hook eye. Wrap the braid up the shank, tie off, and clip the excess.

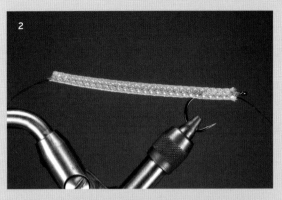

Remove the hook from the vise. Thread the hook through the tubing so the front of the body will end behind the hook eye, as seen in the photo. I didn't have the gold thread specified in Joe O'Clair's recipe, so I threaded a few pieces of gold Flashabou through the tubing; I used a long, looped piece of 30-pound-test monofilament as a threader.

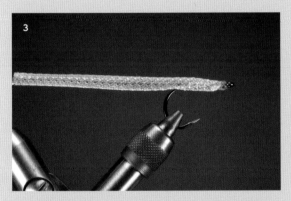

Restart the thread behind the hook eye. Tie off the Flashabou or gold thread and clip the excess. Push the tubing forward and tie off. Tie off the thread and clip. Coat the thread knot with cement.

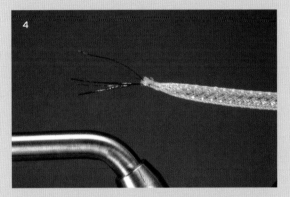

Tie off the end of the tubing. Tie off and clip the thread. Coat the knot with cement. Clip the tail to length.

(tying steps continue on the next page)

Color the body with permanent markers.

Place an adhesive eye on each side of the head. Seal each eye with a small dab of epoxy.

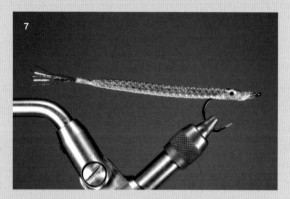

Here we see the finished Realistic Sand Eel, ready for fishing.

# 10

Nantucket with the Heyers

*W*hen it comes to fishing the water around Nantucket, I think the distance and the ferry ride to get to the island create a barrier in the minds of most striped bass fishermen. Why else would such a great fishing destination receive so little attention or press? But, if you have the time to travel and like to sample new fishing opportunities, you should put a trip to Massachusetts' Nantucket Island near the top of your to-do list.

When you go to Nantucket, you should drop in and visit with Captains Jeffrey Heyer and Lynne Burchell Heyer. This wife-and-husband guiding team own Cross Rip Outfitters, a full-service light tackle and fly shop. They also guide, and book charters for several other very experienced charter captains on the island. Whether you wish to fish by boat or the beach, Cross Rip Outfitters can line you up with the right guide.

With respect to tying flies, Lynne is the master of the Cross Rip vise. She's an expert tier, and creates patterns to match the unique fishing conditions found around Nantucket. Curiously, most of her patterns are designed to sight fish for bass on the massive sand flats that surround the island. But, before we started talking about her flies, we discussed Cross Rip Outfitters and the services she and her husband offer anglers. As I discovered, they have a full and varied program.

"Yes, we have a store," Lynne said. "It's Cross Rip Outfitters. It's dedicated to fly and light tackle fishing. But it is a full-service fly shop; we have it all. We've had the shop for eleven years. Jeff and I actually met at a billfish tournament, and once we got married, we moved to the island from New Jersey. Jeff always wanted to have his own business. He had worked in a store that was more marine oriented, and he was just getting into fly-fishing. There were some tackle shops on the island, but none really carried a lot of fly-fishing equipment. That's how we found our niche. At the time, we were all fly tackle, and we also recommended a lot of local guides. After a couple of years, Jeff got his captain's license."

How many guides operate out of Cross Rip Outfitters?

"There's Jeff and myself, and then we have a handful of other guides that we work with. Our op-eration is kind of unique. A lot of the boats in the harbor don't do light tackle fishing, but that's what we and our guides specialize in: fly and light spin fishing. There's another harbor on the west end of the island called Madaket. There's maybe a dozen boats that work out of there, and they're all small; the largest is maybe twenty-six feet long. They're generally all light tackle and fly."

Being on a small island, I guess you can always move around and get out of the wind.

"A lot of the time, yes we can. The only time we really get weathered out is if there's a Nor'easter because of the way the winds shoot down both sides of the island. But a lot of times we can tuck in here and there, and keep fishing."

In addition to using boats, I saw on your Web site that you also have guides who specialize in beach fishing.

"Great Point is a beach fisherman's paradise. The whole beach is connected to Nantucket. You have to have the beach sticker to drive out there, and it's four-wheel-drive. There's a sticker required specifically for Great Point, and then there's another sticker for the rest of the island. If someone is coming out to the island, they should check in with us first and we can advise them on what they need. Sometimes, they might only need the sticker for Great Point. It depends upon the weather and where the fish are located, but we can give them a heads up."

When does your fishing begin?

"Generally, our season begins around the fifteenth of May. The stripers are usually already there and established, so occasionally we'll start around the twelfth of May. If someone is on the island and wants to fish, and if we know the fish are here, of course we'll take them out, but the real season doesn't begin until around the middle of May.

What kind of stripers do you get first? Are they large or schoolies?

"The smaller fish start hitting the south shore of the island first. If you look at a map of Nantucket, you'll see two ponds on the south shore. Those ponds are really full in the spring from all the rain and snow. They seep out fresh water, and the little fish like to go in there to feed on the herring and other things that are attracted to the fresh water. They hit that south shore area first, and then work their way around each end of the island and start moving into the harbors. This starts around the end of April and early May. The big fish start showing up about the first week of May."

How late in the year do you fish?

"We keep guiding until about the twentieth of October. Last year I had a charter for the twenty-third of October, but we got weathered out. The season usually comes to an end around Columbus Day. We don't lose the fish, we lose the customers. But after Columbus Day, if the fish are there, we'll still take someone out."

Do you do any night fishing?

"All of our charters are scheduled around the tides. There are a couple of spots that we like to fish at night, but if that's not happening, I'll suggest that the client do something else."

How big are your tides?

"Between two and six feet. That's not too bad, but it's enough to make a big difference in determining where you fish."

Do you do any sight fishing, or is it blind fishing?

"Almost all of our fishing is sight fishing. That's really Jeff's thing. He runs a twenty-one-foot Pathfinder that's rigged with a poling platform. It's perfect as a flats boat. He can pole flats, or run down the south shore to fish for bluefish."

Really, you do a lot sight fishing? I thought Nantucket was mostly rocky.

"No, we have white sand flats. If you look on a map, you'll see that there are two islands near Madaket. On the north side of these, there are sand flats. These are big ribbons of flats with small channels. And there's a sand bar on the outside of the beach which is really good fishing. There are eelgrass beds on the inside of our harbors; this is blind casting, but it can be very good early in the season. You can pole your boat inside the harbors, or you can drift."

How deep is the water on the flats?

"Some of the flats are dry at low tide, but when we're fishing, the water is between three and four feet deep."

What's the major bait on the flats?

"Crabs and maybe sand eels, but crabs are the predominant bait."

Do you fish the flats in the sun, or do you prefer overcast conditions?

"The only time you can see the fish is in the sun, just like down in Florida; you have to have some sun to see the fish. And it's just not worth it to be out if you can't see anything."

Do you get many clients who only want to fish from the beach?

"Absolutely. Some people get seasick. And some just like the challenge of fishing off the beach. Some people just aren't into the boat fishing, but they love the beach. The beach trips are usually very early in the morning; that's when those guides like to get out. The tides don't seem to matter too much, not until you get into the bonito and false albacore runs. Now, the guides don't like fishing from the beaches at night. I know from my experiences, I always feel like I'm into sea weed or something, but it's dark and I can't tell. Fly-fishing at night can be tough. The beach guides might start fishing from four-thirty to five in the morning, but that's going into the light."

Doyle's Dazzler

Let's talk about your flies. Tell me about Doyle's Dazzler.

"That was created by a guide named Paul Doyle. The fly is now sold by Umpqua Feather Merchants. It's a variation on a Clouser, of course, but it's very popular."

I'm not familiar with Paul Doyle.

"Paul was a fishing-crazed person. He guided in the summer, and did things like floor sanding and

*Chernobyl Shrimp*

painting in the wintertime. He was a great guy who passed away about eight years ago. Paul was a guy who liked fishing at night."

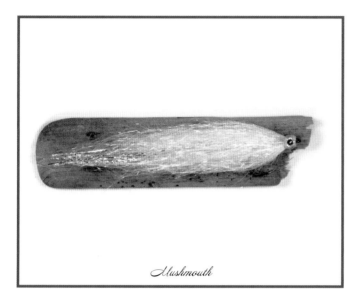

*Mushmouth*

And of course you use the Mushmouth. That's become a very popular fly.

"The Mushmouth has really taken over from the Clouser. I don't know what it is about that fly, but it really works, especially the yellow and the blue. The tan is also very good. I guess that pattern in those colors just about covers most species of bait, but it's a really hot fly. We sell a lot of the yellow, which looks green in the water. Sometimes, when you look at a sand eel in the water, it looks green."

*Blind Crab*

What type of lines do you use for most of your fishing?

"Mostly intermediate and full sinking lines. Sometimes we'll use floating line for night fishing, and those Ghost Tip lines are pretty good. A Ghost Tip line has a ten- to twelve-foot-long intermediate-sinking head, so it's still easy to pick up off the water."

What are your favorite flies for fishing the flats?

"The Blind Crab and the Chernobyl Shrimp are good sight fishing flies for the flats. Those flies are also good for fishing certain spots on the outside of Great Point. Sometimes the guys will see the fish running along the beach, and you're basically sight fishing to them. But you should have good luck with any sort of mole crab type of pattern. During the summer on nice days you'll see the stripers in the water, and even the beach fishermen can target them."

The "Chicken Fly" is a fun name for a fly.

*Chicken Fly*

"The Chicken Fly is an excellent striped bass pattern, but it also works well on bonito; a yellow Chicken Fly is perfect for catching bonito. It's not a big pattern for the flats, but it works pretty well around the rocks in the estuaries."

What fly would you select for fishing moving water?

""We use that squid pattern around the rips. It works best in deeper water around the rocks, so we'll fish that fly with an intermediate or full sinking line. It's really designed for fishing in the rips and moving current."

What kind of bait do you have inside the harbors?

"Herring, anchovies, and mummichogs are in the eelgrass, as well as grass shrimp. We get silversides later in the season."

As we talked about the varied fishing opportunities on Nantucket, Lynne told me about an unusual honey hole that offers a variety of our favorite game fish.

"Have you heard about our Bonito Bar? Between Madaket and Tuckernuck, there's an opening. Outside the opening, maybe a mile or so off the beach, there's an outer sand bar that you have to cross to get out to the ocean. There are a lot of sand bars and rips that line the edges of this chute. When you get on the outside of the chute on the incoming tide, the bait stacks up on the outer bar. You can anchor there during late July and early August, into almost September, and bonito run back and forth along the edge of this bar and chew on the bait. There'll also be bass and bluefish. Later in the fall you might find albies running through, but they like the dropping tide better."

Do you ever fly-fish for tuna?

"Yes, we do get tuna on the fly. We get customers who want to do this, and we have a great time. But it's a seasonal thing, and some years are better than others. Some years they come in close, and some years they don't. But we have some captains who run

*Simple Squid*

larger boats and can go out after them."

What time of the year do you fish for bluefish?

"The bluefish show up some time in mid- to late May. They usually stay along the south shore of the island all summer long, and then we have them until October. It all depends upon the temperature of the water. Sometimes you see the bluefish finning on top, and you can actually sight fish to them. Other times, we'll tease the bluefish up with plugs, and people can cast flies to them. That's cheating, but it can actually be a lot of fun."

Nantucket is quite a tourist destination. How are the accommodations?

"You really have to book in advance, especially during the summer. But there are hotels and B & B's; Nantucket is a huge tourist town. There are a lot of places to stay. It can be expensive during the tourist season, but if you can come during the week, or early in the season or during the fall, it's much more economical. The B & B's are especially nice; they have a much more local feeling. If anglers would give us a call, we'd be happy to give some recommendations."

It was March when I spoke with Lynne, and she and Jeff were in Florida, guiding for the winter. I asked her to tell me about their Florida guiding program.

"The Keys is kind of a small operation where Jeff does all the guiding, and I just sit at the fly tying bench and keep the Nantucket business organized. Our Nantucket guide service is the main attraction, but of course we hope our clients will follow us down to Florida to fish. We actually have one customer who lives down here as well as on Nantucket; she books one day a week with us when we're in Florida, and then she also books one day a week when we're on Nantucket. The customers who like to fish with Jeff up at home also like to fish with him down here."

Where are you located in Florida?

"We live in Duck Key, which is about halfway down. We fish from south Key Largo to Seven Mile Bridge, and then back up to Sandy Key and the mainland of Florida."

I've spent time in Florida during the winter, and know that sometimes the wind can make it hard to fish. How does the wind affect your fishing?

"It was pretty windy this season, so we spent an

awful lot of time exploring. We haven't been able to do that in a long time. We found a lot of new redfish and snook spots, which was a lot of fun."

When do you guide in Florida?

"We guide down here from February until about the middle of April. Sometimes it can be windy, but during February we've had some great bonefishing. And if you get a calm day, you can get a shot at a tarpon. It all depends upon the weather, but that's just fishing anywhere."

## Chicken Fly

**Hook:** Mustad 34007, size 2/0.
**Thread:** Yellow Danville's Flat Waxed Nylon or clear monofilament.
**Tail:** White and yellow saddle hackles—you may add a grizzly hackle dyed yellow on each side—and strands of silver Flashabou.
**Body:** Pearl Bill's Bodi Braid.
**Wing:** Yellow bucktail.
**Belly:** White bucktail.

## Chernobyl Shrimp

**Hook:** Tiemco 37007, sizes 2 to 2/0.
**Thread:** Chartreuse or yellow Danville's Flat Waxed Nylon.
**Tail:** Tan Polar Fiber or Craft Fur Plus barred with a brown permanent marker, with strands of extra fine silver flash material.
**Hackle collar:** Yellow, brown, grizzly, or chartreuse.
**Eyes:** Small painted dumbbell.

## Mushmouth

**Hook:** Tiemco 600SP, sizes 2 to 4/0.
**Thread:** Yellow Danville's Flat Waxed Nylon or clear monofilament.
**Midline:** White Super Hair and silver Flashabou Tie the materials to the hook, and coat the first half of the Super Hair and flash material with Softex. The Softex stiffens the midline and keeps the material from fouling around the hook.
**Back:** Yellow Wing n' Flash.
**Belly:** White Wing n' Flash.
**Note:** This pattern was developed by guide Dave Skok.

## Simple Squid II

**Hook:** Mustad 34007 or Tiemco TMC600SP, sizes 2 to 4/0.
**Thread:** Clear monofilament or Danville's Flat Waxed Nylon in a color to match the fly.
**Tail:** Steve Ferrar's Flash Blend (white, pink, or lavender), but you can substitute with a material such as Bozo Hair blended with fine pearl Flashabou.
**Body:** Pink or pearl Estaz under EP Sparkle, blush pearl.
**Eyes:** Large silver dome eyes glued to the sides of the head.

## Blind Crab

**Hook:** Mustad Big Game Light, size 2.
**Thread:** Orange or pink Danville's Flat Waxed Nylon.
**Tail:** Natural or chinchilla rabbit strip, orange Silli Legs and brown bucktail. The rabbit strip also forms the back of the fly.
**Body:** Tan EZ Bug.
**Eyes:** Orange or tan dumbbell.

## Doyle's Dazzler

**Hook:** Mustad 34011, sizes 1 to 2/0.
**Thread:** Chartreuse Danville's Flat Waxed Nylon.
**Tail:** White bucktail and strands of gold Flashabou.
**Wing:** Chartreuse bucktail.
**Eyes:** Large gold dumbbell with silver adhesive eyes.
**Note:** This is a very flashy version of a Clouser Deep Minnow.

# 11

## Southern Maine
## with Capt. Eric Wallace

e're getting close to the end of our tour of the Atlantic Striper Coast. Now we'll visit with Capt. Eric Wallace, who fishes the rocky coast of Southern Maine. He uses a flats boat, which is an unusual vessel in Maine waters. Whenever possible, he sight fishes to the bass. Capt. Wallace can spend hours perched on the poling platform, pushing the boat over the mud flats in search of big bass. He has miles of water to patrol, so no matter the conditions, he can almost always get his clients into fish.

"I'm fishing Casco Bay. Several rivers flow into Casco: the Presumscot, the Royal, the Cousins, the Little, and the New Meadows River, which is to the north end of the bay. I launch off my trailer most of

the time, but I often go out of the Yarmouth Boatyard. It's just a very convenient place to meet clients. That's at the mouth of the Royal River."

Okay, we're getting to the northern end of the Striper Coast. When do you start fishing?

"I usually get going some time around Memorial Day weekend, and end about the first week or so in October. Sometimes I've had some of the best fishing in mid-October, but this year I was on Cape Cod guiding by October tenth."

Are the first bass of the season large or small? What type of bait do you get early in the year?

"The small striped bass show up first. As for early season bait, we get large herring and alewives. By mid-June, especially in the lower parts of Casco Bay down toward Portland and the Presumscot and Royal Rivers, we get some shots at big fish. But the first round of bass is usually small fish."

How large are those herring and alewives?

"Oh, that big bait is in the ten- to twelve-inch range. After the alewives, you'll get blueback herring."

Do you get blitzing fish early in the season?

"Early in the season, around mid-June, we get blitzing fish on really small bait. They are feeding on tiny alewives and herring, and little micro stuff. The bass key in on it for a couple of weeks. This is when we'll use poppers, but I really prefer fishing some sort of small baitfish pattern right under the surface."

Do they push the bait up against the shore and into the estuaries?

"The fish herd the bait up to the shore, into the estuaries, and even in between the islands. What makes Casco Bay so neat is having so many islands and more than twelve-thousand acres of mud flats. The bait gets pushed up by the bass on the dropping tide and it has to go somewhere, so it'll go into a channel in the mud flat, and this will turn into a giant feeding lane right on the edge of the flat. The fish will just sit there and go crazy for hours! We can get surface action on a sunny day in June until the tide stops."

Capt. Wallace continued to explain the importance of the mud flats to fishing Casco Bay.

"That's one of the coolest things about Casco Bay—there are acres and acres of mud flats. The bait

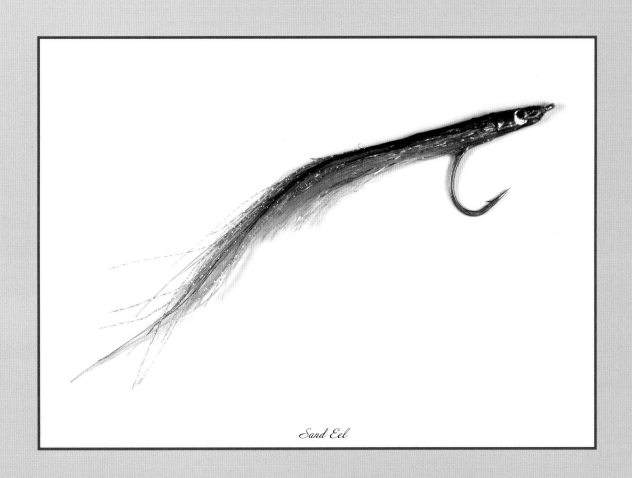

*Sand Eel*

*Seaductive Slayer*

*Seaductive Slayer*

tries to get up there, and the warmer mud will increase the water temperature—even when the rest of the bay is cold—just enough to turn on the bass and kick them into a feeding mindset."

When do the bigger bass start showing up?

"You'll start hearing rumors of people catching big fish between June tenth to the fifteenth. I catch fish in mid-May, but they're small so I don't start offering guided trips until Memorial Day. The fish show up a little earlier than people think, especially in Casco, which gets warmer earlier than other parts of the coast of Maine. I've caught fish at the bridge over the Cousins River on May third, which is very early."

So, how big do the stripers get in your area?

"The biggest fish is between thirty-eight and forty-two inches long. We get a few of these every year, and we catch these fish up on the flats."

What kind of flies do you use mid-season.

"A lot of times the bass key into crabs, but my Seaductive Slayer has become my go-to fly for fishing throughout the season. It's like a flats Deceiver. Just cast it in there, and wiggle it and give it a lot of action. I tie it in a lot of colors. It's derived from the flies of two tyers I pay attention to. One is Ken Abrames with his Flat-wing patterns, and the other is Bob Popovics and his Hollow Fleyes. I tied Hollow Fleyes at one time, but I kept running out of the really long bucktail I needed to make those patterns, so I started adding saddle hackle to create the length. Most Seaductive Slayers are three to five inches long, but when I'm fishing deep down around the rocks with a sinking-tip line, I'll tie it in more of a pollock color and make it seven or eight inches long. And then I do an all-black Seaductive Slayer that is up to a foot long, if I can get the right saddle hackles and bucktail; this is a nice eel pattern. I use a size 2/0 hook for almost all these flies; when I'm fishing the really skinny water, I might drop down to a size 4 hook to reduce the amount of slap when the fly hits the water. It's almost like fishing to a laid up tarpon: Cast the fly in front of them, wiggle it, and let it stay high in the water column. I don't want the fly to dip into the water column too quickly."

Other than tying it in the colors of a pollock, does the Seaductive Slayer imitate any particular type of bait?

"When it's stripped through the water, the silhouette mimics the standard-sized baitfish that we have these days, which is three to five inches long. But, when it opens up, it has a lot of wiggle and action. The feather tail really moves."

I agree: the Seaductive Slayer has a lot of action in the water.

"I've gone through stages of epoxy, and color, and this and that, but the flies got really rigid. I think they're boring to the fish, and they're boring even to me. You get stuck on one thing: matching the silhouette. Well, let's gets groovy, let's get some motion.

"Bucktail naturally pushes water and throws off a little vibration because it's a tad rigid. The Seaductive Slayer opens and closes and pulses in the water. Striped bass have a phenomenal ability to detect vibrations in the water, and if they don't see the fly, they feel or hear it. And then the Seaductive Slayer has the little wiggling tail, so the fly is just there for them."

*Casco Bay Crab Cake*

Tell me about the Casco Bay Crab Cake.

"I tie the Casco Bay Crab Cake in both felt and closed-cell foam. I really like the felt because you can use it to really control the sink rate by just dipping the fly in the water, and then you can bust it out with one cast. You can control it better if it's a little saturated. We have opportunities for sight fishing in two ways. The bass will come up onto the flats for green crabs and sand eels. There is one clear water flat that creates unbelievable opportunities for sight fishing. But with respect to the crabs, it all depends upon the time of year. This fishing is best when the crabs are molting and soft; the bass just love to suck them down. You can find it happening all summer, but I see it more in July."

How did you learn to sight fish to bass on the flats?

"When the water starts to clear in the spring, I can see things from the poling platform that the average fisherman cannot see. Being more of a shallow-water guide, I started paying attention to the fish and the bottom. I started noticing little puffs in the mud, and then a fish cruising over to look at it. This was in four to five feet of water. Then, one day we lost a rod and reel overboard. I said I was going in to get it. Well, it was the incoming tide, so I knew I could walk up the flat and the boat would drift to me. I got up into about ten inches of water, and I could see the backs of fish. The next thing I noticed was that the bass were eating crabs. It was two o'clock in the afternoon, and the fish were in there sucking down crabs. They would feed, then exit the flat, and then come back up. I watched it for three or four days and learned how to fish to it."

Do you sight fish to specific bass?

"Sometimes we get that opportunity, but when these fish are on the flats, they are very attuned to vibrations and noise—even a fly line landing on the stripping deck. Basically, you'll have groups of three or four traveling fish, and one of those fish might turn and look at the fly, but one might not. There are opportunities to find large fish sunning themselves up on the flat. You don't find that all the time, but it can happen. This year, I caught my largest fish in eighteen inches of water."

Your Sand Eel is a fishy-looking pattern.

"I use a lot of Angel Hair and Midge Flash. The head is a piece of lead tape, but I wanted to create a fly that would land on the water softly at the end of a long leader; that's a little different mind-set from your average striped bass fisherman."

What's the story behind the Anti-Clouser?

"I tie the Anti-Clouser just because I got bored tying regular Clouser Deep Minnows. I wanted to do something a little different at the vise. There's nothing

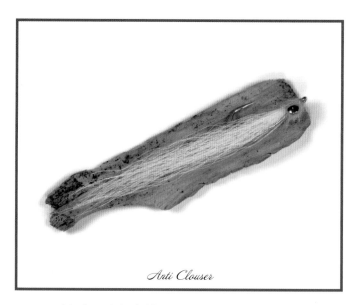

*Anti Clouser*

wrong with the original Clouser; I just wanted to tie something different. It's a general attractor pattern. It's easy to tie and catches plenty of fish. I've taught this pattern in fly tying classes where I needed something simple but different.

"A lot of my flies are based on the fact that I don't have a lot of time to tie. I have twin daughters, and I also get up most mornings around four o'clock to get ready to take clients fishing. I needed simple flies that work, and that's the Anti-Clouser."

*Sand Eel Mushy*

Your Sand Eel Mushy is another sand eel imitation. It has a nice transparent quality.

"The Sand Eel Mushy is a takeoff of Dave Skok's Mushmouth, just a little thinner and with a little less

*Silverside Dropper*

*Grass Shrimp*

profile. It's more eel-like. It's mostly tied using Ultra Hair and Angel Hair. I tie on the Ultra Hair, and then dip my fingers in water. Next, I apply a small amount of Zap-A-Gap to the Ultra Hair, and then quickly spread the glue on the Ultra Hair. This makes the fly slightly rigid and gives it some body. I also wanted this fly to be very transparent like a real baitfish."

The Light Silverside Dropper is an unusual fly. I think it might be the smallest pattern in the book.

"The Light Silverside Dropper is a pattern of Capt. Jeff Becker, who fishes out of Montauk. It's actually one of his albie patterns, but it works perfect as a dropper behind a popper or Gurgler. If you're getting swirls behind your topwater fly, tie this on using a twenty-inch-long piece of monofilament. You will definitely get strikes. Look, when you live in an area that is so dictated by tides, and you can't always get customers to go fishing when the tides are right, you've got to be able to catch fish under tough conditions such as bright sun. I know plenty of guys who won't fish at two in the afternoon under a bright sun, but I have a family to feed and I've found ways to fish under these conditions. This dropper catches fish under even the worst conditions."

What other adjustments can you make to match tough conditions?

"Late in the season, for instance, if the baitfish are jumping out of the water in front of feeding fish, I might use a slightly smaller version of the Seaductive Slayer. I might also go to a fly with a little more flash. But I also like flies on which I can quickly clip off the flash."

Do you have a lot of grass shrimp in your area?

"Yes we do. I got the idea for my Grass Shrimp pattern while watching a guy clean out a fish. The thing was full of grass shrimp. In the morning, you'll see bass that almost look like trout sucking emergers; they're cruising along, and you see the swirl. But there are no balls of bait or blitzing fish, they are sucking down shrimp at the base of estuaries."

I know you also guide anglers to bluefish When does this action start?

"I don't even start thinking about bluefish until July, and the bigger blues start showing up around July fifteenth and then through August into early September."

What other type of guiding do you do?

"During the winter, I guide in the Florida Keys between Marathon and Key West. It helps fill out the season."

### Grass Shrimp

**Hook:** Regular saltwater hook, size 6 or 4.
**Thread:** Black 6/0 (140 denier).
**Eyes:** Small dumbbell.
**Tail:** Olive marabou and strands of pearl Krystal Flash.
**Body:** Black Crystal Chenille.

### Casco Bay Crab Cake

**Hook:** Regular saltwater hook, size 4 or 2.
**Thread:** White 6/0 (140 denier).
**Eyes:** Melted brush bristles.
**Feelers:** Pearl Krystal Flash.
**Weight:** Large dumbbell.
**Legs and claws:** Tan rubber bands.
**Belly:** Tan foam.
**Back:** Olive foam.
**Note:** Use permanent markers to add realistic markings.

### Anti-Clouser

**Hook:** Regular saltwater hook, size 4.
**Thread:** White 6/0 (140 denier).
**Tail:** White and chartreuse bucktail, and strands of pearl Flashabou.
**Eyes:** Large dumbbell.
**Head:** Yellow rabbit dubbing.

### Sand Eel Mushy

**Hook:** Regular saltwater hook, size 4.
**Thread:** Clear monofilament.
**Body:** Pink, yellow, light blue, and black Angel Hair with strands of olive Krystal Flash.
**Head:** Lead taper, cut and folded over the front of the fly to form a solid looking head.
**Eyes:** Small silver adhesive eyes.
**Note:** Coat the head and first half of the body with Softex or a similar product. This keeps the body from fouling around the hook.

## Spike Mac

**Hook:** Regular saltwater hook, size 4 or 2.

**Thread:** Clear monofilament.

**Body:** Pearl and olive Angel Hair.

**Eyes:** Small chartreuse dome eyes.

**Note:** Coat the pearl Angel Hair that forms the belly of the fly with Softex or a similar product.

## Light Silverside Dropper

**Hook:** Short-shank saltwater hook, size 6.

**Thread:** Clear monofilament.

**Body:** White and pink Angel Hair or another brand of soft synthetic hair blended with flash material.

**Eyes and mouth:** Permanent marker.

**Head:** Softex or a similar product.

## Seaductive Slayer

**Hook:** Regular saltwater hook, size 2.

**Thread:** Clear monofilament.

**Tail:** Saddle hackles and strands of Flashabou.

**Body:** Bucktail tied in the Hollow Fleye style.

**Note:** You may tie this versatile pattern in a wide variety of colors.

# 12

Spey Rods, Striped Bass, and Capt. Doug Jowett

e'll end our trip along the Atlantic Striper Coast with Capt. Doug Jowett. Doug is a good friend, expert guide, and very accomplished tier. Although he hails from my home state of Maine, he spends a good deal of the season guiding on Cape Cod. This makes him useful to us because he can give us good insights into fishing in both Maine and on the Cape.

Capt. Jowett is also known for something else: He was one of the first anglers to see the value in using a Spey rod for catching striped bass. Long before the fly rod manufacturers hopped on the two-handed-rod bandwagon—they've almost all added batteries of Spey rods to their catalogs over the past couple of years—Doug was using these extra-long weapons to catch stripers. He's a unique tier and angler, and what he says is based on many years of hard-earned experience.

"I live in Brunswick, Maine, right on the New Meadow River," Capt. Jowett said when describing where he fishes. "It has very good fishing. It's the eastern part of Casco Bay. Right around the corner is the Kennebec River, of course. But the New Meadow has all kinds of islands, inlets, flats, deep water, rips—anything you can think of."

So, you guide on the New Meadow?

"Yes I do. But you have to understand, it's not a real river. It's an estuary that parallels the Kennebec River for about fourteen miles. I have a private dock right at my home. I haven't been on the Kennebec itself for more than a day or two for several years. It just got so crowded over there."

You have two guiding programs. You guide in Maine as well as on Cape Cod. Where do you start guiding first?

"I start on Cape Cod around the first of May. I fish all of the Cape except for the southern tip; I

don't fish that at all. And I don't get over around Provincetown except during the tuna season. I don't go by vehicle, I go by boat from the Plymouth area. But I'm actually based in Falmouth, Massachusetts, because it's so centrally located. I can be on Buzzard's Bay, I can go over to Martha's Vineyard, and I can go up to Cuttyhunk or over to Barnstable."

You're hitting a lot of territory.

"Oh gosh yes. I know it well enough so that if the wind is blowing from a certain direction, I then go to another area to fish. I can always get out of the wind. It doesn't make any difference which way the wind is blowing; we can get out of it."

When did you originally start guiding?

"I've been a full-time guide in Maine for about twenty years. I actually started guiding back in the late sixties, but that was just part time—hunting and fishing. And the fishing was mostly on fresh water. I got into fly-fishing on the ocean by accident. One day I was fishing the Mousam River, and the fish were in real heavy. The next day I said I was going to try it with a fly rod. That was around 1963. I was catching schoolie stripers on a fly rod, and one guy thought I was the hottest spook in the world! I was using a cane rod and a Micky Finn streamer. I can remember it as clear as a bell. That was the beginning of it all for me."

When did you decide to start guiding on the Cape?

"That was around 1990. I had been fishing down there by myself, and I was living in Maine, just starting my guiding business on the salt. Here I was sitting, with all the equipment and time, just wasting away the month of May, so I decided to give it a try down on Cape Cod. I was already guiding on the salt in Maine, I just wanted to extend my season. I did very well business-wise, and fishing-wise, so I decided to continue fishing down there in September. That was before the false albacore frenzy hit, and that became a real boon for light-tackle, small-skiff fishing guides. But I spend the entire summer up here in Maine, fishing mostly for striped bass. We also attack the bluefish—when they attack us."

How long do you stay on Cape Cod in the spring? When do you start fishing in Maine?

"I come back to Maine between the tenth and fifteenth of June. I'm on the Cape for about a month and a half in the spring, and then for about a month and a half in the fall."

When do the bass start showing up in your part of Maine?

"The bass are already here when I return. But the same is true for the Cape; the fish are already there when I arrive, and it just keeps getting better and better with the migrations. And the fish get bigger and bigger as the month of May progresses. By June, the big fish are there. Of course, it all depends upon the migration patterns. There are always a lot of fish around the first of May, but not a lot of fishermen. A lot of guys don't even realize that there's good fishing to be had, especially by boat. It's historical for them to fish the beaches during the early season; they don't even put their boats in until around the first of June. So we have an awful lot of water available with few other fishermen."

What sort of bait do you get on the New Meadow River?

"Early on we get the alewives, just like the entire southern part of the state. Sometimes, depending upon the season, we'll have the dropout of the smelt fishery; they're dropping out of the rivers, going back to sea. They'll mix in with the alewives. We also get some squid. And of course we get the mackerel, but that doesn't start until a little bit later."

How are the menhaden (pogies) holding up in your area?

"The pogies are starting to revive. We're getting both adult and young-of-the-year pogies. We're getting quite a few more, and they're mixing in with the other bait."

When do they arrive?

"It's crazy. Sometimes they show up in the middle of May, sometimes they don't show up until July. But the last few years we've been seeing more and more adults."

I love Maine, but to be honest, it usually doesn't rank high on the list of places to fish for striped bass. You and I know that's a mistake because we have excellent fishing, lots of access to the water, and the scenery can't be beat. Where do your customers come from?

"My customers come from all over the world. I even have a fair number of people from England. I have six or so guys who come all the way from California. I get a fair number from the Deep South; they're trying to get away from all of that heat and humidity during the summer. They're regular customers; they come up every year. I'm very fortunate; I have ninety-percent repeat business. I've been really lucky."

Tell me about fishing Cape Cod during the fall. When do you return to the Cape?

"I go back the day after Labor Day. There are reasons for my schedule. One of the biggest is housing; I'm there during the off-season when it's less expensive. I've got a great deal at the place where I stay, but I also bring them a lot of business and they know that. Otherwise, it wouldn't make a lot of financial sense for me to be down there.

"I stay down there until the wind blows me out, usually around the end of September. Sometimes I'm down there until around the tenth or fifteenth of October, but that's only every few years. Once the low-pressure fronts start coming up through during the fall, they get into a pattern of coming once every ten days. It'll blow for two or three days, that'll stir up the water, and the fishing is lousy for the following two or three days. You'll get five days out of the week that you can't fish, or you certainly can't charge people to fish. It doesn't take long to add up those figures, so I just come home. As soon as I see the weather patterns developing in a certain way, I call my scheduled clients and let them know that the

AP Rattle

fishing may not be very good, or that we might not even get out on the water. They basically make the decision for me. I give them the opportunity to cancel; I don't want to take advantage of anyone."

Let's talk about your flies. Tell me about the A.P. Rattle.

"I wanted a small fly that had rattle in it. There are certain fishing conditions where I like using a fly with a rattle in it. Most of my rattle flies are all big; some of them are really big. Then when this EP Fiber came out, I thought it would be just the ticket for tying a small rattle fly. I tie the rattle right on top of the hook, and the EP Fibers hide the rattle. The A.P. doesn't stand for anything in particular; I just sort of like it."

Is the A.P. Rattle supposed to imitate any particular type of bait, or is it just a general attractor pattern?

"It's just a general attractor pattern."

What time of year would you use the A.P. Rattle?

"I use that fly any time there are schoolies around—fish that are generally up to about twenty-four inches long. And I use it any time the water is dirty or murky after heavy rains."

Do rattles really make a difference?

"I know they do. Years ago, I was on a flat in Maine, and I could see five or six really nice striped bass. I had thrown quite a number of different flies at them, but they wouldn't do anything; they weren't feeding, and they sure weren't interested in my patterns. They were just milling around. So, I tied on a rattle fly, and cast in the opposite direction of the fish—almost 180 degrees from them. I let the fly sink just a little bit, and then I tightened my line. I stripped the fly three times really hard, and I could see the fish getting really nervous; they started circling around and moving real fast. I made another cast to the same area, gave the fly a couple of strips, and continued watching the fish. Just as soon as that thing started rattling, they started swimming in the direction of the fly. Now I couldn't see the fish, but I made a third cast. This time, on about the second strip—bang!—the line went tight. I didn't see the fish, but I was convinced that it was one of those bass that had been swimming in the direction of the fly. They went looking for the rattle. That was very, very vivid to me;

*EP Herring*

*Maine Mackerel*

the whole thing happened right in front of me. Since then I've used a lot of flies with rattles.

"Rattles work well with some flies, but not with others. I have one monster popper that has a rattle in it. It's made of foam, and I put a rattle in it. I swear by that fly. I cast it with a Spey rod; it's the only thing that will cast it. I don't use it all the time; it's kind of a specialty fly. Rattles get fish curious; they get them to come. But if it's a feeding frenzy, you don't need that sort of stuff. And you don't need them early in the season, but they sure do make a difference during the summer doldrums. They are also helpful when there's a lot of fishing pressure and the bass are lying low, or when they're doing a lot of nocturnal feeding. The rattle activates them. There's no question in my mind."

Hey, in your recipes you sent, you refer to the James Bond hook. What does that mean?

"That's the Mustad 34007. Get it? The '007.' I always called it the James Bond hook!"

I've never thought of that. That's unique.

What time of the year do you use the E.P. Herring?

"The E.P. Herring is a good fly for very early spring. And then I don't use it again until maybe August when the herring are dropping back to the ocean."

Your Maine Mackerel Fly is a really nice pattern.

"That's obviously a mid-summer fly for when the mackerel begin to show up."

What type of lines do you use when fishing with streamer-type patterns?

"A large amount of my fishing is done with a 425-grain Cortland Quick Descent head with an intermediate running line. Even when fish are on the surface feeding, you can always pick up better fish underneath. But it really depends upon the anglers, some guys don't want to throw that type of line all day, but that's what I recommend. We fish a lot of structure, and I like to get deep around it. You want to get down to where the fish are."

You have one fly called the Holstein. What's that about?

"It's like the cow. Get it?"

Sorry, but I don't.

"Well, the Holstein is probably my number one go-to fly. I probably use that more than any pattern in my fly box. That fly is basically just a beefed-up

*Holstien*

Deceiver with an epoxied red head. A friend of mine came up with that fly, and he wanted to call it Cow Killer. Sure, some people are going to love the term 'Cow Killer,' but I said he needed to be a little more sophisticated. 'Well, I like that,' he said. He is sort of a rough-sounding guy, you know, and he said, 'What would you call it?' And I said, 'Well, why don't you call it Holstein.' He liked that idea, and so that's what we call it: Holstein.

"The Holstein is a really nice fly. It's easy to tie, and you can make it in a lot of different sizes. I usually tie it in black, as well as the chartreuse and white. Those are about the only colors I use."

When would you use the black version?

"I'm not a big night fisherman, but I'll use it on very foggy mornings; you know, those almost pitch-black, foggy mornings. I also use it in the mid-summer, especially at first light. But I'll always take that black fly off as soon as the first ray of light hits the water. Then I go to the chartreuse-and-white Holstien or another lighter-colored pattern."

You use hot glue to tie the pattern you call the R2-T2. Do you use a lot of hot glue in your tying?

"Yes, I use a lot of hot glue on the body, head, and eyes of that fly. I've become a big fan of using the hot glue gun and yak hair. As you can imagine, you can tie that fly in a variety of densities, as well as a variety of sizes and colors. It's nothing very fancy, but it is a good pattern and also holds up well when bluefish hit it."

*R2-T2*

Having a good sand eel pattern is important for catching striped bass. You tie the Circle Sand Eel.

"There are a lot more sand eels on Cape Cod than in Maine. There are times in Barnstable Harbor, all the way through Cape Cod Bay, especially in late summer and early fall, when the sand eels get really thick. Sometimes the big fish get very selective, just like trout, and if you have a small sand eel pattern, you'll just catch more fish. It doesn't matter if you throw a live eel out there, the bass will just literally ignore it. They want that small sand eel. That fly works well on Cape Cod, but it's also great for fishing in Maine."

Let's talk about using Spey rods. You're well known for using Spey rods when fishing for striped bass.

"Yes I do Spey rods. I use everything from six-weight all the way up to fifteen-weight Spey rods. I love them. I use them on the beach as well as when I'm in the boat."

Is this overhead casting, or do you also Spey cast?

"Both. When I'm in the boat, I'll anchor where there's a good current, and it's just like fishing in a river. I use the same Spey-casting techniques I would use on a river. I'll use a 650-grain sinking head and big herring patterns. You can cast that entire line with no effort whatsoever."

How many years have you been using Spey rods?

"I've been using Spey rods for twelve or fourteen years. I started using them because I was having prob-lems with my shoulder and elbow, and Spey casting is so effortless."

Just as I thought we were concluding our interview, Doug pointed out that we hadn't discussed one of the flies he sent.

"Hey," he said. "What about that Maine Lobster fly?"

What about it, I said. I thought you sent it as a joke.

"Oh God no, that's a really good fly, but it's very specialized. I use it for no more than forty-five minutes during slack tide. It doesn't matter whether it's high or low tide, but I do prefer the low tide when the big fish are concentrated. But you have to fish it at slack tide when there's no current. Any current will flop it over. You want the fly to go to the bottom, and then you just twitch it lightly. I'll cast it into a hole where I know there are probably some good fish, and I'll stay there for forty-five minutes until the tide starts moving. That's it. Nine times out of ten I won't hook up, but on that tenth time, I'll nail a really big bass. I know people laugh at that fly, but it really does work."

### A.P. Rattle
**Hook:** Mustad 34007, size 1/0.
**Thread:** Red Flymaster Plus.
**Rattle:** Large glass rattle.
**Tail:** White EP Fibers.
**Body:** Blue and green EP Fibers with strands of rainbow Krystal Flash.
**Eyes:** Medium gold adhesive eyes coated with epoxy.

### Circle Sand Eel
**Hook:** Eagle Claw Circle Sea Hook, size 2/0.
**Thread:** Clear monofilament.
**Tail:** White FishHair.
**Body:** Olive FishHair topped with rainbow Krystal Flash, and two strands of silver Flashabou.
**Gills:** Red FisHair.
**Eyes:** Small silver adhesive eyes.

### R2-T2
**Hook:** Tiemco TMC600SP, sizes 1/0 to 3/0.
**Thread:** Chartreuse Flymaster Plus.
**Tail:** Two chartreuse schlappen feathers, tied to

*Circle Sand Eel*

*Maine Lobster*

flare out, over strands of silver holographic Flashabou.

**Body:** Yellow Estaz.

**Wing and throat:** Yellow yak hair.

**Head:** Yellow Estaz coated with hot glue.

**Eyes:** Large gold adhesive eyes.

**Side flash:** Gold Flashabou.

**Note:** You can tie this fly in a variety of colors and sizes, and dress it heavy or sparse.

## Maine Mackerel

**Hook:** Mustad 34007, sizes 1/0 to 4/0.

**Thread:** Red Waxed Flymaster Plus.

**Body:** White saddle hackles with black Krystal Flash, and grizzly hackles dyed dark green.

**Nose:** A bunch of green Flashbou tied on, wrapped around the hook, and coated with epoxy.

**Eyes:** Large doll eyes.

## EP Herring

**Hook:** Tiemco TMC600SP, sizes 2/0 to 4/0.

**Thread:** Red Flymaster Plus.

**Body:** White, pink, and blue EP Fibers, strands of rainbow Krystal Flash, flanked on each side with a strand of wide pearl Flashabou.

**Gills:** Red Krystal Flash.

**Eyes:** Large gold adhesive eyes.

## Holstein

**Hook:** Eagle Claw 254SS, sizes 1/0 to 3/0.

**Thread:** Red Flymaster Plus.

**Tail:** Two white saddle hackles on each side with strands of silver holographic Flashabou.

**Body:** Green Sparkle Braid.

**Wing:** Chartreuse bucktail and peacock herl.

**Eyes:** Small adhesive eyes.

## Maine Lobster

**Hook:** Mustad 31010ST, size 6/0 or 7/0.

**Thread:** None.

**Body:** Green pipe cleaners, twisted onto the body, clipped into the shape of a lobster, and epoxied on the bottom.

**Eyes:** Craft eyes.

**Legs:** Grizzly hackles dyed green.

**Antennae:** Peacock herl.

**Note:** As Capt. Doug Jowett describes in our interview, this is not a novelty fly. Under certain conditions, it is one of his go-to patterns for catching large fish. This pattern certainly proves that there's more to fishing for striped bass than casting just Clousers and Deceivers.

# 13

## Capt. Dan Blanton:
## West Coast Striped Bass Guru

The best trout fishing is in Montana, right?

*Then why did the world's-record brown trout come from Arkansas?*

The best saltwater fishing is in Florida, right? Ever see a bluefish blitz on the Jersey shore?

The best fishing for striped bass is on the East Coast, right?

Hold on: Haven't you heard of Dan Blanton?

Dan Blanton is a leading authority on fishing for striped bass in the San Francisco Bay area. His accomplishments remind people who live on the Right Coast that the Left Coast also has great opportunities to chuck flies over the noses of striped bass. After all the hoopla over the East Coast's fishery, it must be admitted that California is also a striper hotspot.

Dan Blanton started fishing when he was young, and converted to fly-fishing early in his career. He is supremely knowledgeable about the history of striper fishing in San Fransisco Bay, especially fly-fishing. Ac-

cording to Dan, there were San Francisco Bay aficionados of the long rod casting to striped bass long before it became fashionable. That's how he knew it was possible to catch stripers on flies: He saw other guys doing it.

(Side bar: When conducting an interview, especially with a fly fisherman, and he gives credit to someone else for coming up with an idea, you know you're talking to a good egg. In this case, when Dan said guys were already catching stripers on flies—that he didn't dream this idea up on his own—I knew he was a straight shooter.)

"I started fishing as a young guy around eleven years old," Blanton said. "When I was a kid, I started fishing for catfish on the Delta, but that wasn't fly-fishing. My dad wasn't a fly fisherman, but my buddy's dad was; he used to take us to the Sierras, and we'd fish for trout with flies. My dad did give me an old bamboo fly rod. He was like a lot of guys who came home from the Second World War with those

bamboo fly rods in the balsa wood boxes. He had one, so he gave it to me. My friend's dad was also a member of a local golf course, and he got permission from the caretaker so that my buddy and I could fish the ponds. I could barely cast past the edge of the weeds, but I'd cast a McGinty Bee and hook big bluegills."

A lot of anglers start out fly-fishing for panfish and trout; for many of us, saltwater fly-fishing comes only after years of tying and casting freshwater flies. Blanton, however, discovered his passion for saltwater fly-fishing at an early age.

"I really became interested in saltwater fishing by the age of fifteen. I started reading about striped bass, and I knew we had stripers in the Bay. My dad worked for the Pacific Gas & Electric Power Company, and he had access to their Antioch power plant. There were guys casting plugs and jigs into the warmwater outflow for striped bass. I made up this nine-foot-long, lead-core shooting head, and tied on a red-and-white Joe Brooks Blonde-style of fly—this was the late nineteen fifties, and the striped bass flies were pretty simple back then. That's how I caught my first striped bass on a fly."

Now, here's where that bit of Blanton honesty works its way into the story.

"I've been credited as being one of the pioneers of fly fishing for striped bass in San Fransisco Bay," Dan continued, "but there were others doing it. People don't know about them, however, because they didn't write about their experiences. But there were other guys, too. I saw them doing it, so I knew it could be done."

Dan Blanton started tying flies more than 40 years ago. Think about it: There were few books, no instructional videos or DVDs, and nothing like *Fly Tyer* magazine. And, of course, this was years before fly fishing clubs or fly shops starting popping up across the country. Where could one go to learn to tie flies? Like so many fledging feather wrappers at that time, he learned the hard way: on his own.

"I didn't have money to buy flies, so I got a cheap vise and taught myself to tie flies. I would take a fly— a Boss pattern or any of the old steelhead patterns— and take it apart and retie it in my mind. I started tying steelhead flies, and sure, they were crude. They

were the simplistic stuff we used on the West Coast rivers back then—the Boss, the Skunk, and all those steelhead patterns. But I eventually learned to tie and created some of my own patterns. A few have become pretty popular for catching striped bass."

If you're a regular saltwater fly fisherman, there's a good chance you've either tied or purchased patterns developed by Dan. He's created a long list of good flies, so we touched bases with only the most popular. Some of these patterns have seen widespread action.

*Flashtail Whistler*

"The Whistler has become my signature fly," Blanton says. "I developed it in 1964 when I was fishing that power plant area. At that time, the fly fishermen were using simple bucktail flies, and they just didn't work as well as the guys who were casting bucktail jigs. The jigs had better action, and I needed to come up with something that would compete.

"I always said I engineered the Whistler. I sat at the vise and said, 'I need a fly that will work and act like a bucktail jig. What will it need to do that?' I used a short-shank, live-bait hook that was made of very heavy wire, and I concentrated all of the weight forward on the hook. I then tied on ⅛-inch bead-chain eyes, and added wraps of lead wire right next to the eyes. I tied the bucktail on so it flared out, and added the red chenille collar to simulate gills. I then made a collar using three or four hackles. The first Whistler was red and white, and it worked just like a

jig, but better: The heavy hackle collar pushed a lot of water to attract fish. The first time I used it, I absolutely slammed the bass and out-fished all the jig guys. Today, the Whistler has caught more than three hundred species of fresh- and saltwater fish around the world."

It would be easy to let the Whistler rest on its laurels, but Blanton continues to tinker and improve his famous pattern.

"Today, I tie all of my Whistlers on sixty-degree jig hooks. [The Mustad 413 is a good example of this type of hook.] Now, no matter how heavily or lightly you dress the pattern, it always rides hook point up, and you never hook fish in the gills. You usually hook them in the sides of the mouth, so you have the benefits of a circle hook, but you get to set the hook. I'm tying almost all of my flies on jig hooks: bonefish flies, tarpon flies, shrimp and crab patterns—they're all going on jig hooks. They ride so much better in the water, and that little sixty-degree bend acts as a lever that really sets and holds the hook.

"I started tying the Flashtail Whistlers in 1971. I was in Costa Rica with a buddy. He was using a pattern called the Lima Bean Jig, and it had strips of Mylar along the sides of the bucktail wing. My Whistlers didn't have any flash at that time, and he was kicking my butt. I came to the conclusion that it was the flash. We didn't have Flashabou at that time, so I tied on strands of Mylar tinsel and then tied the fly. I went back out and just annihilated the fish. I've been tying Flashtail Whistlers ever since."

While the Whistler doesn't represent a specific baitfish, Dan does tie patterns that do. He is, however, partial to flies that work in a variety of situations. The Sar-Mul-Mac is a good example of his utilitarian creativity. Here again, he credits another tier with giving him inspiration.

"The Sar-Mul-Mac is a general imitation of a sardine, mullet, or mackerel. I came out with it in 1971, and consider it one of the forefathers of all the anchovy style flies—all those big-eyed flies. At that time, no was tying anything like it. Bill Catherwood was tying his Giant Killer flies, and he inspired me with his spun deer-hair heads. I use this basic idea to tie almost any large, elongated fly. The main difference is that I use Ultra Chenille for the heads, and

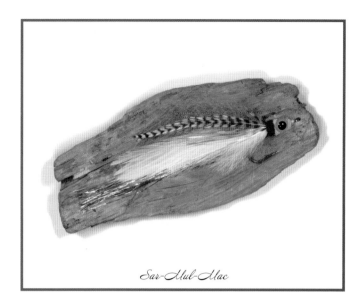

Sar-Mul-Mac

glue on big 9-millimeter eyes. The big heads also push a lot of water."

Don't think that Dan Blanton only fishes the waters around California. While discussing his flies, he constantly told tales of fishing around the world. He also described using some very unusual tying materials.

"I came up with the Punch series flies to imitate small tropical-looking reef baitfish. I use these to fish for snapper in places like the Florida Keys. Later, they became very popular for catching snook, baby tarpon, and a variety of fish. I tie these in a wide range of colors.

"I came up with the Bay Delta Eelet way back in the late sixties. I use it to imitate monkey-face eels

Tropical Punch

*Sea Arrow Squid*

and coastal eels that the striped bass eat. I originally tied it using feathers and black horse mane hair. Horse mane is very durable and sinks well, but today we have lots of synthetic substitutes. I used to resist synthetic materials because I couldn't find anything I really liked, but Flashy Fibre and Kinky Fiber work really well, especially as filler material in the wing and as the underbelly. But I'm still a strong feathers-and-bucktail guy. I would love to tie an Eelet for you, but I'm out of horse hair."

Like his father, Dan worked for Pacific Gas & Electric. When the company downsized, Blanton opted to retire after 30 years of service. He was already publishing articles in fishing magazines and lecturing at clubs, so with a retirement package in his hip pocket and a growing reputation in the angling community, he was able to make an easy transition into the world of professional fly-fishing. Today, he is one of California's hottest striped bass guides.

"I guide from the first of October through about April. That's the winter season on the California Delta where all of our major rivers come together. We have striped bass, salmon, black bass, and a variety of other species. The striped bass come into the system in the autumn to spend the winter. They spawn in the spring, and then drop out of the Bay system. We target them up in the Delta. This is just a wonderful place. It's a wilderness area that has sustained itself despite the massive metropolitan sprawl surrounding it. I guide from a skiff, and on some days we'll cover sixty or seventy miles a day—looking for that dream school, you know.

"The fish can run anywhere from what we call dinks—stripers in diapers—to fish that weigh more than thirty pounds. You never know: one cast is a three-pounder, the next cast is a thirty-pounder. The average fish weighs four to six pounds with the occasional eight to nine pounder, and some double-digit fish."

When not guiding in California, Dan leads trips around the world. Every year, he logs thousands of miles to some of the planet's best fly-fishing.

"I lead trips to Australia, Alaska, Baja, and Canada—I love to do pike and lake trout trips in northern Manitoba. We don't do clinics; it's just very relaxed fishing."

Like all conscientious anglers, Dan knows the importance of protecting our fragile fisheries. He has become an outspoken leader in protecting San Francisco Bay and the Delta region. Every year, he helps raise thousands of dollars for this important effort.

"We've developed a tremendous fund-raiser called Striper Fest. It's a barbeque held on the first Saturday in November, and about 130 guys show up. We raise about fifteen thousand dollars for the Northern California Council of the Federation of Fly Fishers Bay-Delta conservation committee. It's remarkable how it has grown over the past several years, and I'm really happy to help."

### Sar-Mul-Mac (Sardine)

**Hook:** Targus 812 or another brand of standard saltwater hook, size 3/0.

**Thread:** White 3/0 (280 denier).

**Tail:** Silver and pearl Flashabou and white saddle hackles.

**Belly:** White bucktail.

**Back:** Pink bucktail, grizzly saddle hackles, and gray Ultra Hair.

**Flanks:** Pearl Flashabou.

**Gills:** Red chenille.

**Head:** White chenille with two strands of gray chenille folded over the top.

**Eyes:** Extra-large yellow dome eyes.

### Flashtail Whistler

**Hook:** Eagle Claw 413 Jig Hook, size 2/0.

**Thread:** Chartreuse 3/0 (280 denier).

**Eyes:** Large dumbbell eyes.

**Tail:** Silver and pearl Flashabou.

**Belly:** White Kinky Fiber, Big Fly Fiber, or a similar material.

**Back:** Chartreuse bucktail and light blue Krystal Flash.

**Flanks:** Rainbow Krystal Flash.

**Gills:** Red chenille.

**Collar:** White and chartreuse saddle hackle.

### Blanton's Sea Arrow Squid

**Hook:** Long shank stainless steel hook such as the Mustad 34011, size 2/0.

**Thread:** White 3/0 (280 denier).

**Tentacles:** White saddle hackles and rainbow
    Krystal Flash.
**Head:** White marabou.
**Body:** White chenille.
**Fins:** White calftail.
**Eyes:** Large yellow dumbbell eyes.

## Blanton's Tropical Punch
**Hook:** Eagle Claw 413 Jig Hook, size 2.
**Thread:** Orange 3/0 (280 denier).
**Eyes:** Medium dumbbell.
**Tail:** Gold Flashabou and yellow bucktail.
**Wing:** Yellow bucktail, grizzly hackle dyed orange,
    rainbow Krystal Flash, peacock herl, and pea-
    cock Krystal Flash.
**Throat:** Yellow hackle fibers.
**Head:** Orange chenille.

## TIER'S TUTORIAL: *Tying the Flashtail Whistler*

Start the thread on the hook. Tie on a large dumbbell.

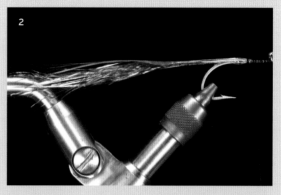

Tie on your favorite colors of Flashabou. Coat the first one inch of Flashabou with cement; this will stiffen the material and prevent it from fouling around the hook while fishing the fly. Allow the cement to harden before proceeding; this takes only a couple of minutes.

Tie a bunch of synthetic fibers to the top of the hook; this forms the belly of the fly. I am using Slinky Fibers.

Flip the fly over and tie a bunch of synthetic fibers on the other side of the hook.

(tying steps continue on the next page)

Tie on your choice of bucktail to form the back of the fly.

Tie on your favorite colors of Krystal Flash. Dan Blanton is generous with the flash, and so am I.

Tie on red chenille or Crystal Chenille, and wrap the gills. Tie off and clip any remainder.

Tie on a large white saddle hackle. Wrap the feather up the hook, but don't crowd the dumbbell. Tie off and clip the excess white hackle. Tie on and wrap a blue hackle. Tie off and clip any leftover. Make a neat thread head in front of the dumbbell. Tie off and clip the thread. Coat the thread with cement. The Flashtail Whistler is a beefy fly for a big, beefy striped bass!

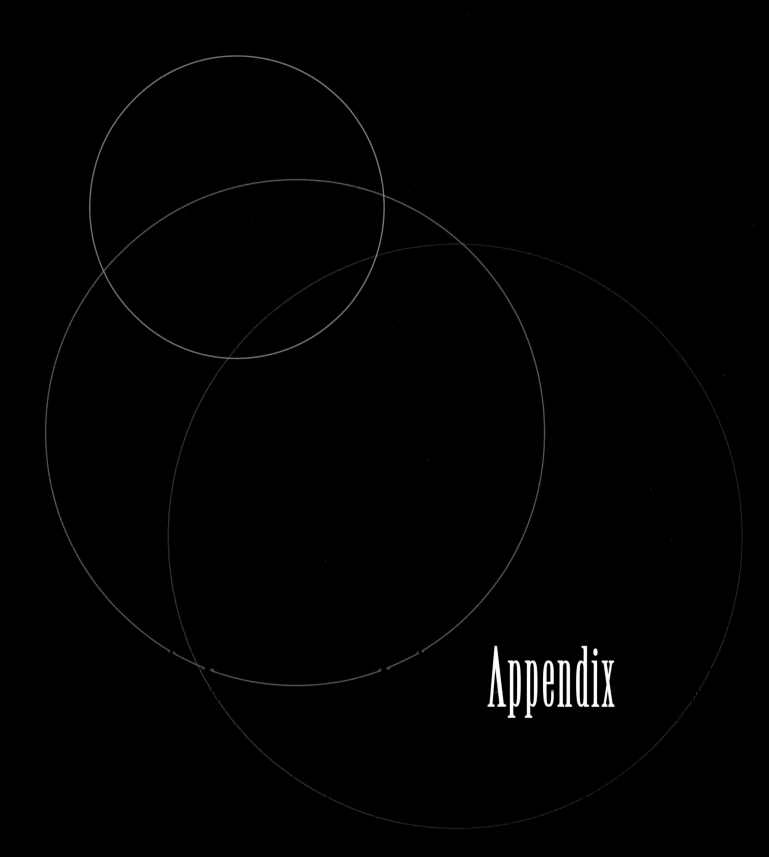

Appendix

# Talk With the Experts

*My thanks to the terrific guides and fly designers who so generously shared their time and patterns with me. They let me pick their brains, and I learned a lot. Use the following information to contact the great folks who appeared in this book.*

**Capt. Brian Horsley**
(252) 449-0562
www.outerbanksflyfishing.com

**Capt. Chris Newsome**
(804) 815-4895
www.bayflyfishing.com

**Capt. Gene Quigley**
(732) 528-1861
www.shorecatch.com

**Capt. Joe Mustari**
(732) 888-9669

**Capt. Joe Blados**
(631) 765-3670

**Capt. Ray Stachelek**
(401) 884-3794
www.castaflycharters.com

**David Nelson**
www.squimpishflies.com

**Capt. Jim Ellis**
(508) 362-9108

**Joseph O'Clair**
www.flycatcherflies.com

**Capt. Lynne Burchell Heyer**
(508) 228-4900
www.crossrip.com

**Capt. Eric Wallace**
www.coastalflyangler.com
(207) 671-4330

**Capt. Doug Jowett**
(207) 725-4573
www.home.gwi.net/~djowett/

. . . and last, but hardly least . . .

**Capt. Dan Blanton**
(408) 778-0602
www.danblanton.com

# Index

redfish, 4, 9, 15, 16, 109
rhea, 73
Rhode Island, 55
Rick (friend), 8, 9
Rick Fink, 41
Rio T-14, 79
Rio T-14 head, 3
Rock Candy Crab, 12, 18
Rowayton, Connecticut, 73
Royal River, 112

*Saltwater Fly Fishing* (magazine), 70
Sand Eel, **42**, **86**, **113**
Sand Eel Fly, 44
Sand Eel Mushy, **116**, 116, 119
sand eels, 84, 85, 105, 115, 128
Sandy Key, 108
San Francisco Bay, 134, 139
Sara Gardner, 2
Sara's Half & Half, 3
Sardine (fly), **63**
sardines, 62–63
Sar-Mul-Mac, 137, **137**
Sar-Mul-Mac (Sardine), 139
Sea Arrow Squid, **138**
Seaductive Slayer, **114**, 115, 119, 120
sea worms, 87
shad flies, 8
sheet foam, 49
shrimp, 38, 85
Shrimp (fly), 1, **22**
Sierra mountains, 134
Silverside, **58**
Silverside Dropper, **117**
silversides (spearing), 12, 38, 59, 85, 108
Simple Squid, **108**
Simple Squid II, 109
skipjacks, 29, 56
smallmouth bass, 73
smelt, 124
snapper, 137
snook, 109, 137
Spartina Grass Shrimp, 12, 18
spearing, 22, 26, 38, 59
speckled trout, 4, 9, 16
Spey hackle, 73
Spey rods, 122, 127, 128

Spike Mac, 120
squid, 41, 59, 60, 62, 84, 124
Squid (fly), **95**, 96, 99
Squimpish Fly, 70, **81–82**, 91
Stachelek, Ray, 55–67
Staten Island, 34
Stealth Wing Streamer, **60**, 64
steelhead patterns, 135
striped bass
    in Block Island, 59
    Chicken Fly used for, 107
    coastal eels eaten by, 139
    Crease Fly used for, 48
    Flat-wings used for, 70
    at Gardiner's Island, 49
    in Maine waters, 124
    in Nantucket, 104
    in Outer Banks, 4
    in Rhode Island, 56
    in San Francisco Bay, 134
    Seaductive Slayers used for, 115
    season for, 2, 9, 27, 29, 56, 59
    in shallow waters, 15
    in southern Maine, 112
    Spey rods used for, 128
    Tuna Melts used for, 86
*Striper Moon* (Abrames), 73
Surf Candy, **26**, **31–32**, 38

Thunder Creek, 86
Tie 'Um High Bunker, 15, 18
Tropical Punch, **137**
trout, 70, 135
trout flies, 73
tuna, 26, 29, 108
Tuna Melt, **86**, 86, 88
tying instructions
    Crease Fly, **54**
    Flashtail Whistler, **141–142**
    Guzzle Bug, **89**
    Half & Half, **5–6**
    Noisy Clouser, **19–20**
    Rabbit Eel, **66–67**
    Realistic Sand Eel, **101–102**
    Squimpish Fly, **81–82**
    Surf Candy, **31–32**
    Worm Fly, **46**

Ultra Bright Rattle Squid, **60**, 62
Ultra Bright Rattle Squid (Purple), 64
Ultra Chenille, 137
Ultra Hair, 63, 119
Ultra Shrimp, **41**
Umpqua Feather Merchants, 49, 105

Vineyard Sound, 84
Virginia Beach, 9

Walburn, Steve, 70
Wallace, Eric, 111–120
Whistlers, 135
Whiting Farms, 79
Whiting hackles, 79
Wool Head Bunker, **41**, 44
Woolly Bugger, 80
Woolly Bully, 14
Worm Fly, **45**, **46**
Worm or Krill Fly, 44

Zap-A-Gap, 119